Career Leap by Michelle Gibbings is an outstanding guide for leaders and individuals to draw their own map to leap up, out or across to expanded or radically different career paths as the future of work in Australia rapidly changes from emergent technologies.

—Anne Bennett
Executive General Manager, NAB

Warning… if you aren't looking for a new career yet, by the end of Michelle's wonderful book you just might be! She packs the pages with tools and inspiration that will have you seeing your own potential. You will be excited, energised and equipped for your next career move.

—Kieran Flanagan
Co-Founder, The Impossible Institute

Taking the Leap is something many ponder, dream about, fantasise over and procrastinate on for months or years. Sadly, some miss the opportunity by allowing it to build into something bigger than it needs to be. I'm the type of person that often takes the Leap and then does the thinking. Michelle's book has given me fantastic insights into what can be defining moments and decisions in your life. If you're considering taking the Leap, stop and read Michelle's book first. I'll think about my next Career Leap differently now having read the book.

—Peter Baines OAM
Founder and Managing Director, Hands Group

Pablo Picasso's famous quote comes to mind, 'Learn the rules like a pro, so you can break them like an artist'. Jam packed full of provocative thinking, actions and ideas, *Career Leap* by Michelle Gibbings does just that. It also shares anecdotes and personal insights of those that have gone before and taken the leap, giving us real-life examples of what IS possible. A must read for all, no matter what age or stage of life.

—Dr Jess Murphy
Founder of Pathway to Your Potential experiential programs
and self-confessed Career Leapist

T0357945

We have all come across highly successful people who have been able to leap from role to role, and industry to industry, leaving a trail of achievement behind them. They seem to be powered by self-belief, adaptability and enthusiasm. In our rapidly changing world this is a skill we will all need to acquire, as existing roles disappear to be replaced by new ones and as entire industries are disrupted.

In this book Michelle clearly identifies how to analyse your existing situation and motivation. She provides a powerful case for personal change, with many examples. More importantly there are a wide-range of practical tools to help you prepare and execute your own career change. Michelle is passionate about helping people to attain career success and anyone reading this book will gain valuable insights and skills to perform their own career leaps.

— Chris Whitehead F Fin
CEO and Managing Director, FINSIA

There are rich veins of gold threaded throughout this book. It's a refreshing and contemporary look into the often daunting prospect of career planning and provides great tools and tips such as the four career health zones which, whilst a tad confronting, is spot on!

If you're seriously looking to invest in your career, are willing to put in some good old fashioned hard work with the promise of delivering tangible results, then this is the book for you.

— Leigh Bryan
Financial services Executive, Suncorp

Disrupt yourself … Michelle provides wise counsel and great tools to help you thrive in (the future of) work. Drawing on her experiences, advice of experts and interviews with people who have leapt in their career, this book provides a handy guide for shaping your own. Love the focus on life-long learning and continual leaping.

— Mette Schepers
Partner, Mercer

It's strange to think that many of us began our working lives in rather less enlightened times when 'job-hopping' was very much frowned upon. Indeed, I remember resigning from my first role after University (because I knew deep down that it wasn't right) and being told by my manager that 'people don't move jobs before they've done 10 years'. Well what a difference a lifetime makes!

And what a difference this book makes. *Career Leap* is an insightful, practical and incredibly useful guide to analysing your current career situation and assessing whether it's right for you or whether a 'leap' into something different is the most appropriate path to follow. Far from advocating a leap in the dark, Michelle advocates a much more considered and thoughtful approach. Changing careers—she argues—is a project that, like all successful projects, needs to be managed closely from start to finish. In this sense, Career Leap is best described as the ideal guide for project managing your career.

The central message of *Career Leap* is one that I find both powerful and incredibly liberating; it's my career and I'm in control of the path that I take. If I know that the path isn't the right one, it's probably time to take a leap. As someone who has 'leapt' a couple of times since that first role after University, I couldn't agree more!

— David Pich MA (Cantab) FIML
Chief Executive, Institute of Managers and Leaders and
author of *Leadership Matters: 7 skills of very successful leaders.*

In the uncertain world that is the new world of work, Michelle has given us a really practical and wise handbook full of clarity, optimism and inspiration. She deftly combines some of the most useful models from diverse research fields, with personal insights and powerful stories from professionals who've excelled at career transitions. Best of all, she provides a practical and accessible step-by-step guide to help you leap with confidence into your new career.

— Professor Richard Hall
Deputy Dean, Leadership and Executive Education
Monash Business School

Career leap is a fantastic read for anyone who's contemplating a leap or change in their career.

Coming from the recruitment industry I can appreciate where Michelle describes the change to our future work with the introduction of automation. It's time to think ahead and differently about our careers and start to future-proof.

I love the approach of the open workbook style throughout allowing you to work through and assess your career re-invention. I am lucky enough to love my work, however in the back of my mind I have considered a career leap for a few years and after reading this book it inspires me to take that leap! Thank you Michelle for the great insight and motivation!

—Jemma Dougall
Regional Director, M&T Resources

In today's fast paced world where we are constantly reading about the future of work, this is a great practical handbook that everyone can use to proactively face these challenges head on, take control and have the confidence to make that 'leap'. For many of us, we take the time to do a health check, but when did we last look at our career? Michelle's 'how fit is your career' health check is a must do for all of us! A highly relevant book regardless of your industry or profession.

—Somone Johns
Head of Business Development, nbn and Commercial Delivery, Telstra

I really enjoyed reading and experiencing *Career Leap*. Having leaped myself a couple of times through my career, Michelle's book really resonated and I found it inspirational. I wish I could have read it sooner as it could have helped me with some of my earlier career choices too, and I will definitely hold onto it.

It's a very practical guide that helps you to get to know yourself better, helps you understand what makes you 'tick', moreover assists you proactively with your choices so you can take charge of your own destiny. The framework and the many tools shared are a must-have as you navigate through your career journey. It warns you of the possible pitfalls, however also gives you the confidence to back yourself, and as you re-invent yourself, you truly feel supported.

Agility has become the new currency, and it's so important to stay relevant on so many levels. This book is a great source equipping yourself for the present and the future, so you can be the one proactively steering on to what's next, and re-inventing yourself along the way.

—**Anouk De Blieck**
Global Senior Human Resources Leader
(Connect on LinkedIn: www.linkedin.com/in/anoukdeblieck)

Career Leap is the concentration of years of accumulated wisdom from Michelle Gibbings—a brilliant practitioner who has taken the leap many times in her career. Michelle is well credentialed to provide invaluable insights on what it takes to build a plan to optimise your career and take a leap forward—from a small step to a seismic shift in career direction.

What I most value about this book is its practical orientation. Michelle speaks directly to the reader about what you can do to future proof your career; through the application of four simple considered stages, you will avoid career stagnation, skills obsolescence and navigate career leaps to help you promote success in work and life.

The pace of change in today's world is blistering and whether by accident or design, change brings both opportunities and rampant chaos. *Career Leap* is a cornucopia of insights and additional website resources to help readers cope with these challenges. It provides tangible and practical examples of career leaps made by successful Australians who share their inspirational stories. Their stories and anecdotes are complemented by a practical guide on how to capitalise on opportunities that come your way.

By reading this book you'll discover new career possibilities, reinvent yourself and put in motion a realistic and achievable career plan. I highly recommend *Career Leap*. Read it and apply the learnings—you will come on in leaps and bounds!

—**Dorothy Hisgrove**
PwC Partner, Chief People Officer

CAREER

LEAP

MICHELLE GIBBINGS

CAREER

LEAP

HOW TO REINVENT AND LIBERATE YOUR CAREER

WILEY

First published in 2018 by John Wiley & Sons Australia, Ltd
42 McDougall St, Milton Qld 4064
Office also in Melbourne

Typeset in 11/13 pt Adobe Garamond Pro

© John Wiley & Sons Australia, Ltd 2018

The moral rights of the author have been asserted

National Library of Australia Cataloguing-in-Publication data:

 A catalogue record for this
book is available from the
National Library of Australia

Cover design by Wiley

Printed in Singapore by C.O.S. Printers Pte Ltd

10 9 8 7 6 5 4 3 2 1

Disclaimer
The material in this publication is of the nature of general comment only, and does
not represent professional advice. It is not intended to provide specific guidance for
particular circumstances and it should not be relied on as the basis for any decision to
take action or not take action on any matter which it covers. Readers should obtain
professional advice where appropriate, before making any such decision. To the
maximum extent permitted by law, the author and publisher disclaim all responsibility
and liability to any person, arising directly or indirectly from any person taking or not
taking action based on the information in this publication.

*To Craig for helping me with my homework, and
to Barney for not eating it.*

CONTENTS

Foreword   *xv*
About the author   *xvii*
Acknowledgements   *xix*
Preface   *xxi*
Leap online   *xxv*
Introduction   *xxvii*

Phase 1: ASSESS: Where are you in your career now?   **1**

1   Check: Are you future fit?   3

2   Realise: What is your potential?   15

Phase 2: ARCHITECT: Where do you want to be?   **37**

3   Explore: What are your options?   39

4   Choose: What will you progress?   57

5   Construct: What plan will you follow?   69

Phase 3: ACTIVATE: How will you get there?   **85**

6   Shape: What is your new career identity?   87

7   Influence: How will you enter the market? 101

8   Focus: How can you make each day matter?   117

Phase 4: ACCELERATE: How will you leap quickly and successfully?   **133**

9   Launch: How will you transition and land? 135

10 Advance: When will you celebrate and what will you do next? 151

A message from Michelle   *159*
Sources   *161*
Index   *165*

FOREWORD

The great challenge of the modern workforce isn't so much finding work, although that can indeed prove difficult for the young and the non-skilled workers. It is steering a way along a tricky pathway that presents many twists and turns along the way.

Work was a straightforward concept in the twentieth century. Everyone was scooped up by the globalisation of the great manufacturing companies both in Australia and abroad. There were jobs aplenty. All you had to do was learn the rules, put your head down, and work day-in and day-out for the whole of your working career.

And that is precisely what many workers did for their entire working lives, whether it was for a car manufacturer or for a professional services firm. It was a process that delivered prosperity but it also set up expectations about how work should be, and that needs to be unravelled by workers in a post manufacturing world.

In *Career Leap* author Michelle Gibbings shines a light on the way forward for workers in the twenty-first century. Gone or going are the great global manufacturers. Long gone is the idea of working in one job for the entirety of your working life. Now in are bold new concepts like digital disruption, globalisation, mechanisation, artificial intelligence and, perhaps most powerful of all, the desire for personal growth and development.

Working on an assembly line might have delivered an assured job from an early age but, gosh, it wasn't exactly a personally fulfilling use of time. The next generation of workers see work differently, and indeed they have to see work differently. The skills now required are far more complex including agility, sociability and self-confidence, and this on top of the need for technical and entrepreneurial skills.

In this masterful and engaging work Gibbings is a bit like the conductor of an orchestra. She draws on research evidence here, on the experience of notable individuals there, on her own insights and experience and even on quotes from famous people in history. Aristotle gets a mention. I even saw a quote from Geronimo.

In many ways Gibbings has constructed a how-to book on career growth and development for the twenty-first century that mirrors the way careers must unfold in the twenty-first century. A bit of this, a bit of that but always with an underlying theme, a rhythm if you like, of personal growth and development and with a watchful eye on prosperity and commerciality.

This is a complex story well told by an experienced story-teller and conductor who adroitly brings in different players to add just the right note at just the right time. I loved this book, not just for its insight into navigating the modern career, but also for the way Gibbings pulls everything together for the reader's engagement and enjoyment.

Congratulations Michelle. *Career Leap* is a great leap forward for anyone navigating work in the twenty-first century!

Bernard Salt AM
Author, columnist, speaker, corporate advisor
Melbourne, December 2017

ABOUT THE AUTHOR

Michelle Gibbings is obsessed with helping organisations, teams and individuals get fit for the future of work.

She has leapt many times in her career—from politics to mining to corporate to business owner; from speechwriter to public affairs advisory to leading compliance and risk functions, to leadership development and career mentor, with many more roles and industries in between.

After spending 20 years at senior levels in the corporate world, Michelle made the ultimate leap to setting up her own consulting practice. Now she thrives on advancing meaningful progress and helping leaders thrive and shine in this complex, changing world.

Michelle has a distinguished reputation across the Asia-Pacific region as a keynote speaker, adviser, facilitator and executive mentor of choice for many leading-edge corporates and global organisations.

She regularly appears across a range of media, including *The Age*, *The Sydney Morning Herald*, *The Australian*, *The Australian Financial Review*, the *Herald Sun*, *Women's Agenda*, *The Huffington Post*, *The CEO Magazine*, *HR Director*, Australian Institute of Managers and Leaders, *Elle*, Mamamia, *Marie Claire*, *Sky News*, *Today Extra*, *Radio National Drive*, Radio 2UE and other syndicated radio stations.

Her first book, *Step Up—How to Build Your Influence at Work*, was released in 2016.

When not facilitating sessions, mentoring, writing or speaking at conferences, Michelle loves to travel from country to exotic country (yes, leaping is a life theme) with her best friend and husband, Craig.

Michelle lives in Melbourne, Australia, with Craig and their dog, Barney.

ACKNOWLEDGEMENTS

The idea for this book had a long gestation period, with many people I've met throughout my career influencing it. It is by seeing what others have done, and through my own experiences, that the ideas in this book have come to life.

A book is never written alone, and this one wouldn't have been possible without the many generous people who helped along the way.

To Ann Crabb, thank you for listening to my early ideas and helping to constructively challenge them.

Thank you to Alicia Beachley, Andrew Wiseman, Christine Bartlett, Christie Kerr, Glenn Brennan, Julian Fenwick, Peter Griffin, Robyn Weatherley and Russell Yardley, who all, without hesitation, reached out to people in their networks to help me secure interviews for this book.

A massive thank you to all the people who so readily shared their thoughts, ideas and experiences about their career leaps, including Andrew O'Keefe, Aneka Manners, Anna Jenkins, Dr Bronwyn King, Christine Bartlett, Clare Payne, Gorgi Coghlan, Helen Silver AO, Janine Garner, Jessica Watson OAM, John Bertrand AO, Layne Beachley AO, Dr Lisa O'Brien, Marc Alexander, Nigel Matthews, Rodney George, Sandy Hutchison, Simon Madden and Steve Bracks AC.

Your generosity in sharing your ups and downs, and your wisdom, have made this book rich with real, tangible and practical insights.

While it was an idea for a long period, the manuscript itself was written in super-fast time. Thanks to Kelly Irving for her amazing work in keeping me on track and making sure everything came together.

Thanks also to Adam Matthews and Drew Blatchford, two amazing osteopaths, who made sure my wrists and forearms survived the writing onslaught, and to Chris Nikola for the PT sessions that helped keep me physically focused.

This book wouldn't be the same without the advice and efforts of the Wiley team. To Jem Bates, Lucy Raymond, Ingrid Bond and Chris Shorten, thank you for helping bring this book to life.

A special thanks too for Bernard Salt for writing the Foreword for this book. His expertise and forward thinking approach to the world of work has influenced many—including me—and I am very grateful to him for sharing his thoughts on *Career Leap*.

Most of all, thanks to Craig for putting up with the many weekends when I was bunkered down in my study writing. You really were the best decision I ever made!

PREFACE

My first career ambition was to be a member of *Charlie's Angels*—that's the original 1970s TV show starring Jaclyn Smith, Farrah Fawcett and Kate Jackson. As I grew up, at different times I thought I wanted to be a librarian, a teacher, a journalist or a lawyer—though I never did get a degree in education (well, not yet) or take the bar exam.

Like many of my friends, after high school I enrolled in a course at university (a Bachelor of Business Communication) because, well, back then it was what you did. You'd do a trade apprenticeship or go to university, which is still very much what happens today. I had no idea where it would take me.

It ended up being the start of a 20-year career that involved working for six different companies, moving to a different geographic zone nine times, getting promoted 10 times, working in seven different functional areas, completing three degrees and eight certifications, being a member of six professional associations, and holding three board positions and one advisory role.

Throughout this time, I took what seemed like large leaps as I moved from one discipline to another, one industry sector to another, one career field to another. I moved from politics to mining to banking, from being a company spokesperson to working on a large project, from working in corporate affairs to working for the CEO.

Often people would ask me how or why I did this. One friend once remarked, 'Michelle, your career *terrifies* me.'

For some of us, these leaps are scary. They seem not just impossible, but *implausible*. I mean, how on earth do you move from being a teacher to a state premier, a lawyer to a TV personality or a banker to a fashion designer? (All are completely possible progressions, as you'll soon see.)

Yet for others, like me, these leaps are born out of a love of learning and challenge. Sometimes our needs or interests have changed or we simply feel we are in the 'wrong role'.

Over time, I have come to realise that making these leaps has actually helped *advance* my career. I learned to take advantage of opportunities as they arose, and to sustain my career when times were tough or challenges arose.

This attitude and approach is, now more than ever, something we all need to embrace.

In this age of robotics and automation, work roles that were once seen as 'secure' over the long term are disappearing faster than new and different roles are being created. The number of us facing redundancy or being forced to move on to new roles continues to increase.

It is up to us to take our future into our own hands.

The upside of all of this change is the new opportunities it brings.

There are amazing opportunities for you to embrace a role that you love, that inspires you, that makes you want to get up for work every day. Perhaps it's a role that uncovers a hidden talent, or provides you with the chance to do truly meaningful work that makes a difference on either a local or a global scale.

If you sit back and wait, these opportunities will pass you by and go to someone else, so it's up to you to do something about it, which is where this book comes in. It will help you:

1. **assess** where you are in your career now

2. **architect** where you want to leap to

3. **activate** how you get there

4. **accelerate** how you leap successfully.

This book does not set out to assess artificial intelligence and its impact on the world, or to offer an in-depth critique of changes to today's workforce — there are plenty of books in the market that do that. Rather, I want to offer an incentive and a source of inspiration that will challenge you to make deliberate decisions in your career, as well as a practical guide on how to take advantage of what the future brings.

I've helped countless people transition into new careers. In *Career Leap,* you'll hear about these people. You'll read their stories and those of others who have successfully made leaps in their careers — for example, from banking to fashion, sport to corporate or public to private sector.

But there is a catch. The strategy I will outline is only effective if you actually do the work, and complete the exercises contained here. They require deliberate time, deep thought and reflection, potentially with the help of a trusted adviser, partner or colleague.

That's why I recommend you print out the exercises and complete them in your own time, and not just once but at different stages in your career.

All of the exercises can be downloaded from: michellegibbings.com/resources

Career success and ongoing employment require you to actively manage your career each and every day. You can't afford to play safe, to stay small, to not take risks, to not change or position yourself effectively. You must continuously develop yourself, constantly look ahead and actively plan your career.

You can jump over a little stream or you can leap tall buildings in a single bound. It's just a question of how high and how far you are prepared to go, and how much risk you are willing to take.

So as you embark on this quest and leap into your brilliant future consider the words of the inventor Thomas Edison, a man who was famously dismissed by a teacher as 'addled': 'If we did all the things we are capable of doing, we would literally astound ourselves.'

That's what happens when you learn to *leap*.

LEAP ONLINE

Whether you are a hard copy or digital book reader, it always helps to have additional online resources to read and refer to along the way. Scattered through the book are many exercises and checklists to help you progress through the Career Reinvention Cycle (which you will learn about shortly) and make your career leap. Supporting these activities are a selection of online resources including worksheets and tips, which you can also download from:

michellegibbings.com/resources

Undertaking a career leap takes focus and effort, and you will need to do lots of thinking and planning. The exercises in this book will help you do just that. If you skim through them, you aren't likely to make as much progress as you would like. By keeping them as a handy reference, you'll be able to refer back to them and track your progress throughout your career leap adventure.

As you'll soon see, making a career leap isn't something you do just once. You'll leap multiple times during your career, at different stages and ages, and for different reasons.

Keep the work you do for this leap easily accessible — it will help you next time, and the time after that. It will be interesting to see what has changed for you each time too.

Enjoy the experience, and make your career leap count.

Michelle

INTRODUCTION

When you land on 'Go' in a game of Monopoly, you collect $200. When you hit a ball that races to the boundary line in cricket, you score four runs. When you serve in tennis and your opponent fails to return it, it's an 'ace', and you win the point.

These are rules of the game. It's near impossible to play successfully if you don't know them. Or if they keep changing, and you don't know they've changed, and you have no ability to influence how they play out.

In life, one of the biggest games we play is work. Depending on what we do and where, there are different rules attached to this game. These rules can be written and unwritten, fixed or malleable, prescriptive or general, helpful or unhelpful.

The rules for your work might require you to be at the office before 9 am, to finish at 5 pm and to take a lunch break at midday. Or state that if you hit your KPIs for the year, you'll get a bonus. Or perhaps that you get a rostered day off each month. Typically, these rules are set by someone else—the person, organisation, industry or government you work for.

To succeed at work and across your career, you need to know not just the rules but how to navigate them (and sometimes when to ignore them) so you can get stuff done.

Many constantly changing external forces are affecting the rulebook of work. How we work and what we do at work are undergoing a seismic shift, mainly thanks to new technology, which is making us more mobile and our workplaces more flexible. At the same time, automation and artificial intelligence are impacting many professions and roles.

The rules of the game, as you once knew them, have changed and will continue to change so rapidly that one day you could wake up and find you don't know how to play the game.

You need to make the new rules work for you, not against you.

Today's challenge

Throughout your career you face decisions on multiple fronts. These decisions are not just important but essential to your future success and ongoing happiness. Regardless of how you feel about your job now, at some stage in the future you'll need to shift, reshape or reinvent your career.

What decisions are you making to future-proof your career?

The term *future-proof* is often used in the technology and medical sectors, where it's crucially important to build products that retain their value and don't quickly become obsolete. It applies equally to your career. If you want to enjoy a long-lasting and interesting career, you need to future-proof it.

Through our work we provide a service, and over time any service, just like any product on the supermarket shelves, risks becoming obsolete and being replaced by something else. Something that's bigger, better, brighter, faster, more innovative.

If you worked in an office in the 1960s (or watched the TV series *Mad Men*), you will recall the pool of secretaries clicking away on their Remington typewriters while managers sat in their private offices, the size of which was dictated by their seniority, using rotary dial phones to make important calls. By the early 1980s secretaries were using electric typewriters, then over time the whole typing pool vanished as each employee took possession of a heavy personal desk computer (no remote working here).

At that point you communicated by fax or, if you were really ahead of the times, a mobile phone the size and weight of a brick. The arrival of email and wi-fi in the 1990s changed all this. As the new century progressed we turned to laptops, BlackBerrys and, finally, smartphones. Now individual offices began disappearing entirely in favour of open, collaborative work spaces and hot-desking, while more and more of us worked from home.

Technology has changed not just how we work, but when and where we work too.

Technology's role as a catalyst for change isn't new. In medieval times, for example, books were handwritten and painstakingly copied by monks, until the fifteenth century when Gutenberg's printing press superseded their work. Today much of our communication is done online, so jobs relying on hard-copy printing have declined while jobs depending on digital devices have increased.

What sets our world apart today is the dizzying pace of change as well as its breadth. Society is approaching a crunch point. The World Economic Forum has dubbed this period of history the Fourth Industrial Revolution, as the fusion of technologies is blurring the lines between the physical, biological and digital. Robotics, nanotechnology, artificial intelligence, machine learning, genetics and biotechnology are coming together to create totally new environments.

Revolution or evolution?

In his best-selling 2016 book *Homo Deus,* futurist Yuval Noah Harari wonders what will happen to the many millions of people who will enter what he calls the 'useless class' as computers take away our jobs. Business leaders, from Alibaba's Jack Ma to Microsoft's Bill Gates, also worry about what these changes will mean for workers.

As Jeffrey Joerres, former CEO and chairman of ManpowerGroup, puts it, 'We must deal with the reality that when full-scale robotics and AI arrive in a broad-based, affordable, easily justifiable way, we'll see enormous waves of workers put out of work and ill prepared to take on different jobs.'[1]

A 2016 report by the CSIRO and the Australian Computer Society, *Tomorrow's Digitally Enabled Workforce,* concluded that nearly half of all jobs in Australia are at risk from computerisation and automation.

Additionally, a McKinsey Global Institute report in 2017 found almost half of today's available work activities have the potential to be automated. Their analysis, which surveyed 46 countries representing about 80 per cent of the global workforce, found that fewer than 5 per cent of occupations could be fully automated using currently available technology. However, about 60 per cent of occupations have at least 30 per cent of activities that could be automated. Their conclusion was that most occupations will change in some way.[2]

Whether you see technology as a force for good or for evil, what you can't deny is that these changes are ushering in a new era for the workforce.

At the Fiona Stanley Hospital in Perth, Western Australia, robots are already dispensing drugs and are reported to be safer, less error prone and more efficient than humans in this role. In Japan, insurance company Fukoku Life is using IBM's Watson Explorer technology to calculate payouts to policy holders. The system will scan hospital records and medical certificates and extract the relevant data to determine the correct payout.

LEGO's factory in Billund, Denmark, is almost fully automated. Precisely calibrated robotic machines create up to 36 000 brick pieces per minute; that's around 2 million pieces every hour and billions every year. And these machines work 24 hours a day. They don't take sick leave or holidays. They may occasionally be shut down for maintenance, which is no doubt carried out by another robot.

In Amazon's vast warehouses, it's estimated that employees spend no more than one minute taking an item off the shelf, boxing and shipping it. The rest of the work is done by robots, and automated processes and systems. Now comes Amazon Go, essentially a retail store with no checkout. With the Amazon Go app on your smartphone, you can just walk in, take what you want and go.

The impact of these changes extends from blue-collar to white-collar employees, manual workers to knowledge workers. If the work involves any process that can be coded into a machine or any task that can be standardised, it will likely be at least partially automated.

If we ignore the reality of change, we will be left behind.

A job for the future

My father was an academic with a tenured position, a permanent post at the university he was employed by for as long as he wanted. He worked there from the beginning to the end of his career. Can you imagine that?

The concept of a job for life no longer exists. The latest statistics in Australia show that most workers are highly mobile, changing jobs every three years. The rate of casual and contract work is increasing. Those entering the workforce now are likely to have at least 17 different employers and five different careers during their lifetime.[3]

Over the years, the nature of the relationship between employer and employee has changed, and loyalty has certainly suffered. The employee provides a service for which the employer pays compensation. Ideally, it is an exchange of equal value. But when that value equation feels out of balance, one party will quit the relationship and move on. As the rate at which this happens has increased, so the length of time an employee stays with the same organisation has dropped.

Charles Handy first introduced the concept of the Shamrock Organisation in his 1989 book *The Age of Unreason*. The Shamrock has three types of workers[4]:

1. a central group of high-value, core employees

2. a group of independent contractors, typically professionals

3. a pool of temporary workers, often on outsourcing contracts, usually doing low-end work.

This idea plays out in the workforce today. Organisations are blending internal and external resources to bring together the right skills more efficiently. In the future, teams will increasingly be self-managed, with employees having no permanent boss. Companies are also moving from having professional managers to what Bain & Company call 'mission-critical roles'.[5]

Organisations won't need as many managers in the future.

In China the Haier Group, a consumer electronics and home appliances company, is built around marketing, design and manufacturing. The teams are fluid, focused on specific projects and sourced through an internal pool of resources. Organisations like this pull workers together for a distinct project, and once the project is finished the workers move on to something else.

Similarly, in Australia the ANZ Banking Group is moving towards a scaled, agile philosophy, adopting a team-based approach to the delivery of work, as opposed to a hierarchical approach.

Already, contingent workers or freelancers make up about 40 per cent of the total workforce in the United States, and this is expected to rise to 50 per cent by the year 2020. The corresponding figures for Australia are 30 per cent and 40 per cent respectively.[6] More than 85 per cent of all new jobs created in Australia in 2016 were part-time or casual.[7]

With borderless teams, co-working spaces and freelancing on the increase, these temporary flexible jobs, coined the 'gig economy', have undermined the traditional economy of full-time, work-for-life jobs. Whichever statistic or source you relate to, there's no denying the impact this is having on our personal and professional lives.

Playing the new game

In the past, the rules of the game were fixed. They were set by big organisations and bureaucracies. Now there is a democratisation of the workforce that enables you to have much more freedom and choice about how and when you work.

The gig economy and the transition to an automated and fully flexible workforce is here! Yet most of us are still completely unprepared for them. We still tend to have an outdated view of what a career path looks like. We are encouraged to think of it as linear: we enter the workforce and explore a few roles, then midway through our career we land something that will keep us happy until we retire.

Careers these days are fluid, organic and adaptive, which means they need a degree of reinvention. Gone is the notion of one organisation and one role or function for life. Gone is the notion that someone will plan your career for you, and you can sit back and just let it happen.

You can't rely on recruiters to find roles for you. You can't rely on your current organisation to develop you. You can't rely on roles finding you. This may sound hyped-up or scary to some readers, but it's a reality that we all need to be prepared for.

Salim Ismail, the author of *Exponential Organizations* and an expert in helping organisations leverage technology and strategy to grow faster, suggests, 'Today, if you're not disrupting yourself, someone else is; your fate is to be either the disrupter or the disrupted. There is no middle ground.'[8]

Now more than ever you need to be comfortable designing and orchestrating your own career path. You need to find roles that work for you, and sometimes you will have to create your own. You must be ready and equipped to embrace change at any moment. You must become the leader of your own destiny, your own career.

> Knowing how to write the new rulebook for your career gives you a competitive advantage that will last long into the future.

So let's recap. Table I.1 shows you how the rulebook setting the parameters of work has changed, and the new possibilities you will want to embrace.

Table I.1: career parameters

Ditch the old career parameters	Create new career parameters
Job for life — a few companies with a number of different roles	Multiple careers — potential for multiple companies, roles and career paths
One role and one company at a time	Portfolio of roles — jobs on the side, side hustle or 'moonlighting'
Full-time or part-time employment with hours relatively fixed	Flexible work arrangement that suits your lifestyle and needs
Job taker: you take the job that is on offer	Job maker: you create your own job that fits your lifestyle, skills, competencies and ambitions
See yourself as working in a 'role', which has no defined end date	See yourself as working on a 'project', with a more defined start and end date
Manage your career, which has a linear progression	Own your career, which has a circular progression with multiple points of career reinvention
You are hired because of your formal knowledge and qualifications.	You are hired because of your life experience, expertise and competencies.
You rely on recruiters, job advertisements and your reputation to get a job.	You rely on your network and market positioning to get work. It's the value you deliver that matters.

Value your work

In their book *The 5 Patterns of Extraordinary Careers*, James Citrin and Richard Smith map out the three phases of a linear career:

1. **Promise** — from formal education to early thirties

2. **Momentum** — from mid thirties to early forties

3. **Harvest** — from forties to retirement.

In phase 1, your *perceived value* was significantly weighted towards your potential or promise. As you moved into the next phase your potential value was converted into *experiential value,* as you mastered skills, took on more responsibility and built your credibility through experience.

By phase 3 you had been in the workforce for 25 to 30 years. At this point your career either plateaued or declined, or if you were well positioned it continued to advance. The authors give the examples of people who advanced to board roles, consulting engagements, and not-for-profit or broader advisory roles.[9]

In such a linear career world certain rules to career success applied. You were told to get a trade or university degree, to work hard and specialise. It was your skills and hard work that would help you achieve your aspirations. You were encouraged to discover what you were passionate about. You may have worked for a business or organisation, or been self-employed, and for many your company was your brand. You looked ahead and planned your career by seeking direction, with a 10-year career plan in hand. Your work had a defined start and stop time frame, which was set by your boss or the person you worked for.

Today, it's all about value. The value you can deliver to others through the work you do. But what is valued changes over time, just as the value of currencies in foreign exchange markets fluctuate and new currencies enter the market.

To future-proof your career it's essential to know the value of what you offer—your market value—and to be able to increase that value and, at times, change it.

The Career Reinvention Cycle

Regardless of where you are or how you feel about your work now, at some stage in life you'll find you need to shift, reshape or reinvent your career—and you'll need to learn to leap.

The catalyst for this change will be one of the following:

- **Choice**. Your needs or interests have changed and you've decided to do something different. You *want* to move on.

- **Conscription**. Your role has been made redundant or has changed significantly. You are *forced* to move on.

Many of us feel uncomfortable with change, particularly if we believe it is being 'done to us'. The Career Reinvention Cycle, illustrated in figure I.1, is designed to help prepare you for whatever the world throws at you, at any age and at any stage of your career. This need or desire to leap won't just happen once. It will happen multiple times, which is why it's a cycle.

The cycle involves constantly scanning the horizon, seeing what is changing and determining how you need to respond and position yourself for the next stage of your career. The Career Reinvention Cycle will guide you through the key actions you need to take to make a successful leap onto a completely new career path at any time in your life.

Figure I.1: the Career Reinvention Cycle

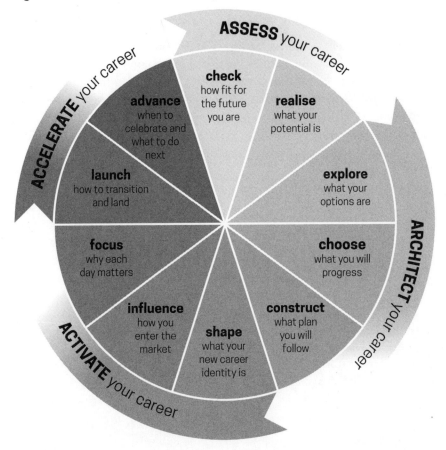

Many people have made career leaps, and in doing so have redefined their career options and liberated their career outcomes. The Career Reinvention Cycle will help you to do this too.

Phase 1: Assess where you're at in your career now

In phase 1, you'll get real about where you are right now. In much the same way as you would when joining a gym, you will put your career through a fitness assessment. This will help you understand how fit your career is for the future. You'll start to equip yourself for the future by identifying what could hold you back or constrain you from making a leap.

Phase 2: Architect where you want to leap to

In this phase, you'll start to explore the realistic options you have for making a leap. You'll examine your strengths and skills in the context of how the world of work is changing. You'll be asked to make choices and tradeoffs to create clear, actionable next steps and to develop a plan to get to where you want to head.

Phase 3: Activate how to get there

In phase 3, you'll take the plan you have created and start putting it into action, getting ready to go to market. You will make decisions about how to position yourself, build the right network and manage your exit from your current role. Your influence and go-to-market strategy is crucial to enabling your leap.

Phase 4: Accelerate how you leap successfully

In the final phase, you will transition into your leap. There are certain elements to consider when your leap is 'in flight', to ensure you land successfully. Leaping doesn't stop there, of course. You need to learn to stay one step ahead of the game, and this phase will show you how.

PHASE 1
ASSESS
Where are you in your career now?

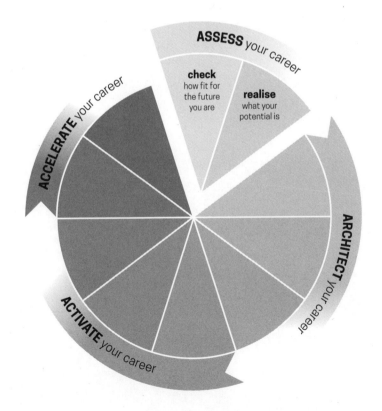

ASSESS your career

check
how fit for
the future
you are

realise
what your
potential is

ACCELERATE your career

ARCHITECT your career

ACTIVATE your career

Your career is just one piece of the big pie we call 'life', so you need to examine it in the context of everything that affects you externally and the decisions you are willing to make internally.

In this first phase, you're going to assess your career as it stands now and where it could be in the future. You'll identify what impacts your choices, including family, colleagues and individual circumstances.

Just as you have a regular medical check-up, you need to periodically check up on your career. How fit are you to leap? Have you been oiling the machine or have you been cruising, watching too much TV on the couch, eating potato chips and letting things get away from you?

Through this process you'll start to identify your individual constraints and, more importantly, where there are opportunities. So let's lose the remote control. It's time to get fit for the future of work!

1
CHECK
ARE YOU
FUTURE FIT?

*'Ambition has one heel nailed in well, though she stretch her fingers
to touch the heavens.'*
Lao Tzu

For some of us, work is a necessary evil, to be endured in return for money so we can pay bills, go on great holidays and fund a lifestyle—it's a means to an end and nothing more. For the fortunate few, it's something we love doing. Work gives us purpose, satisfaction, enjoyment and fulfilment.

Love it or loathe it, work is a critical part of your life.

Across your lifetime, you are likely to spend up to 100 000 hours at work or in some form of employment. That's based on you starting full-time work at 18, retiring at 65 and working only eight hours a day for the standard 261 working days of the year. If you are a workaholic or are used to putting in a few hours of overtime each week, it's likely to be substantially higher.

So wouldn't you rather be doing something you actually like to do?

I don't mean you'll like every minute of every day (that's totally unrealistic), but on balance you find it stimulating, interesting and valuable. Something you feel good about getting up for instead of hiding under the doona.

Many of us feel trapped in a job we don't like. We're bored, in a rut, stressed out or overwhelmed by the sheer volume of work we need to do. And yet we remain in that rut, telling ourselves, 'Yeah this place sucks, but better the devil you know. At least I know how this place works.' Or, 'I don't know what else to do. It's too hard to find a new job.' Or, 'I can't afford to go — this place pays too well.'

Does any of this sound like you? If your work makes you so unhappy that it impacts not just your wellbeing, but those around you, then it's time to consider 'voting yourself off the island'. That means taking control and making the decision to go somewhere else or do something different, even if it feels hard or uncertain.

> Yes, finding work can be challenging, but a job doesn't just provide financial benefits — it's also critical for our self-esteem and mental health.

There's no doubt there will be points in your life when throwing in a job could feel like an irresponsible luxury. There's the mortgage, school fees and bills to pay. It's not a luxury, though, when you're working in an environment that is eating away at you, impacting your behaviour, destroying your self-confidence, and causing undue stress and anxiety. If you don't change the environment, it will slow you down, block you or stop you in some way.

CAREER STOP SIGNS

Change is hard, which is why so many of us stay in jobs we hate until something (or someone) forces us to move on.

Here are six warning signs that it may be time for you to cast that vote:

1. **Your performance is dropping.** Your work environment no longer brings out the best in you. Your motivation is low so you only do what you have to do. This 'bare minimum' approach is impacting your performance, the outcomes you deliver and ultimately your reputation. This type of damage can have long-term consequences, including making it even harder to get that next job.

2. **Your values are misaligned.** Your values and those of the organisation are out of alignment so you feel like you have to change who you are when you are at work. This may show up as your not feeling comfortable voicing your opinion, or finding yourself forced to support ideas that go against what you believe in.

3. **You now have 'cynic' as your middle name.** You spend large parts of the day complaining about what's happening at work. You don't trust your work colleagues and you no longer offer ideas on how to improve things. You only complain about them.

4. **You are constantly worried you are next in line.** Your workplace is forever restructuring and making people redundant, and you are constantly worried about when the axe will fall on your role. You can see that technological change is going to consume your job.

5. **You're on the brink of burnout.** You feel burnt out and the physical signs of stress are presenting in how you behave at home with your friends and family. You feel exhausted all the time and the thought of going to work makes you feel anxious or highly emotional. You dread Monday morning, and likely drink several glasses of wine or beer in the evening to drown out the day.

6. **You've stopped learning.** You don't feel like work is challenging you. You're bored or uninterested by what's going on. You feel like there's no more room to grow or expand your horizons. You need something else to push you so you're not always working on autopilot and counting down the clock.

How many of these conditions can you relate to? All, none or some? If it's all or some, it's time to seriously think about overhauling your career. It's time to change and get in shape!

Find new cheese

In his classic business parable *Who Moved My Cheese*, Spencer Johnson tells the story of two mice, Sniff and Scurry, and two little people, Hem and Haw. The mice and the little people lead a comfortable if predictable life, taking the same route each day to the store of cheese on which they feed. One day, however, they discover all the cheese is gone.

Sniff and Scurry had been noticing the gradual reduction in the cheese store and weren't surprised. They moved on quickly to find a new source of cheese. Hem and Haw, though, found the change very hard. They felt entitled to the cheese and had become lazier and less inclined to put effort into finding a new source. All of this made it much harder for them to adapt when the change hit.

They became nervous and unsure about how to respond to the changed conditions. After much pain and struggle, they eventually found an effective way to respond and ultimately to find new cheese. They learned many lessons along the way, a pivotal one being that they needed to 'smell the cheese often so you know when it is getting old'.[10]

There are many people who, like Hem and Haw, don't know how to react to change and specifically how to respond when their job changes or disappears. This is a very real problem, because all our jobs are being impacted at some level by new technology, artificial intelligence and automation. And this is why you need to learn to leap and reinvent your career, at any age or stage.

> You must look ahead and plan so you don't wake up one day and discover all your cheese is gone.

Change is hard, but it doesn't have to be so. All you need to know is how to find new cheese. The only difference between you and someone who has made a career leap—from lawyer to media personality, sailmaker to corporate leader or sports star to investment banker—is that they were intent on finding new cheese.

These leaps didn't happen by accident. They were planned and involved deliberate decisions and targeted actions. They reinvented their career step by step, which is what you're going to learn to do.

Is a robot coming for your cheese?

We are all being impacted by technological change and automation. The two questions to ask yourself are, 'How much am I being impacted?' and 'What does this mean for me?' Your answers will help set you up to take advantage of new opportunities as they arise.

There are a number of different ways to do this. Online tests will indicate broadly how much of your job is likely to be impacted by automation. Google 'future proof quiz' and you will find a range of options, such as the quiz created by WorkingNation, a nonprofit organisation based in the United States (visit futureproofquiz.workingnation.com). It is focused on raising awareness of the workforce employability gap created by advances in technology and globalisation. Googling 'will a robot steal my job' will also lead you to a variety of resources, including willrobotstakemyjob.com.

These explorations can help you to gain clarity on how 'safe' or 'vulnerable' your current role is.

It can be easy to ignore how the world is changing and to lull yourself into a false sense of security, but the chances are you will be affected by these changes. It's better to be aware and prepared, rather than remaining in denial. The more prepared you are, the more options you will have.

How fit is your career?

Doctors advise us to get an annual medical check-up to make sure we are physically healthy and in good order, but when was the last time you put your career through a fitness check, to see if everything is on track for the future?

Your career warrants the same level of attention as your health because the two are closely connected.

A career health check isn't just relevant to people who aren't enjoying their work or working environment. It's important for everyone who is in the workforce or trying to re-enter the workforce, particularly in the context of the rapid change we are facing in today's world.

We all need to understand whether our career is fit for the future. Assessing it periodically helps you determine whether you are in a rut or holding on to an unrealistic, outdated view of your career. It also challenges you to think about what may need to shift and what you may need to do more or less of to ensure a successful, sustainable and rewarding career.

Exercise 1.1 (overleaf) is your starting point for building a plan to future-proof, reinvent and ultimately liberate your career.

Exercise 1.1: Check your career health

Answer yes or no to each question in this table.

Part A: time focus		Yes	No
1	Do you spend time actively planning the next steps in your career?		
2	Do you believe your role/profession will change significantly in the next three years?		
3	Are you aware of how your role will be impacted by the arrival of new technologies such as AI and robotics?		
4	Do you continually stay abreast of how your industry and profession is changing?		
5	Are you clear on the value you offer through the work you do, and how that value may need to change?		
6	Are you taking regular steps to build your knowledge base and network?		
7	Are you looking for ways to improve the work you do, rather than doing it the same way it's always been done?		
8	Have you taken deliberate action in the past 12 months to update your career profile and position in the market (such as updating your LinkedIn profile, meeting new people or engaging in profile-building activities)?		

Action: For each 'yes', give yourself one point. Tally your score (with a maximum total of eight points).

TOTAL

Interpreting your results for Part A

If you scored 5 or less in this exercise, you are *past* focused. If you scored 6 or more, you are *future* focused.

For Part A, write down if you are past or future focused.

Now answer yes or no to the following questions.

	Part B: career focus	Yes	No
1	Are you willing to take risks with your career and move into roles where you feel uncomfortable because you don't (yet) have all the skills and knowledge?		
2	Do you believe your career success is the direct result of the effort you put into it?		
3	Do you believe you can influence your career outcomes?		
4	Do you spend money and time on career and personal development, including in areas beyond what is needed for your current role?		
5	Have you proactively built a network to support your career progression?		
6	Do you maintain a balanced perspective on your employability and career prospects (i.e. not overly anxious or overly ambivalent)?		
7	Do you believe it's your responsibility (not your employer's) to develop yourself and your skills?		
8	Do you critically assess and reflect on your career progress at least once a year?		

Action: For each 'yes' you answered, give yourself one point. Tally your score (with a maximum total of eight points).

TOTAL

(continued)

Your zone of health

Depending on how you've answered the questions in this first exercise, you will fall into one of four career health zones, as illustrated in figure 1.1.

You can work out what zone you are in by looking at your results from Part A and Part B of the exercise. Part A is your position on the vertical axis and Part B is your position on the horizontal axis. Find the points of intersection to locate the career health zone you currently occupy.

Figure 1.1: the four career health zones

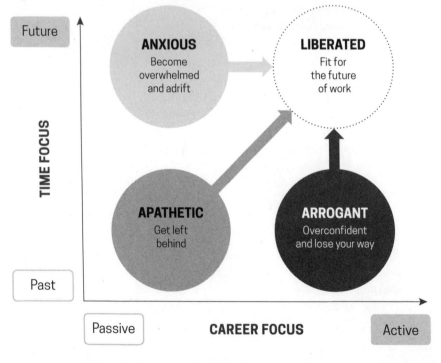

10

The four health zones can be summarised as follows.

Zone 1: Apathetic (passive approach, past focused)

If you're in this quadrant, you typically make choices and construct a life that makes you feel like your career options are limited. You are so focused on the past and just living for the moment that you spend no time preparing for the future. You rarely engage in deliberate career development and career decision making, preferring instead to rely passively on options suggested by others or expecting others to manage your career for you. Ultimately, you are getting left behind.

Zone 2: Anxious (passive approach, future focused)

In this quadrant, you let fear drive the decisions you make—fear of failure, fear of the unknown, even fear of the future. You make easy, less risky career decisions and are more concerned with what could go wrong than with seizing possible opportunities. Your future focus is stunted by a passive acceptance that you can't change or influence the outcomes. Ultimately, you are getting so overwhelmed that your career is drifting.

Zone 3: Arrogant (active approach, past focused)

Here you are extremely confident of your place in the present because of the success you have had in the past. Consequently, you don't take a long-term view of your career. You ignore the fact that the world changes, and so too does your place in it. While you may consider yourself to be actively focusing on your career goals, you fail to devote enough time and energy to developing and reshaping your skills and competencies to ensure you are future ready. Ultimately, through your overconfidence you lose your way.

Zone 4: Liberated (active approach, future focused)

Equipped with the willingness, knowledge, insight and skills to implement a sustainable future career, you enter the liberated zone. You balance delivering in the present and focusing on what the future may bring. You see yourself as the architect of your own career, and take deliberate and focused steps to stay ahead and position yourself for growth and advancement. Ultimately, you are prepared and ready to take career leaps to sustain a successful and fulfilling career.

Find the next chapter
John Bertrand AO

John Bertrand AO will always be remembered for his critical role as the skipper who led Australia to victory in the America's Cup in 1983.

'I was wondering what to do next after the America's Cup,' he says. 'I rang up the then Prime Minister, Bob Hawke, and asked him to introduce me to the most entrepreneurial person in Australia. He asked me if I could be in Sydney the following night to meet Sir Peter Abeles.

'This led me to a corporate career with Ansett Energy, which was a high-tech startup between Israel and Australia focused on solar energy development. From there I moved into the world of finance and property development. After that I launched a company on Nasdaq, which was a partnership with NBC focused on sports broadcasting over the internet. I now sit on a number of boards and am President of Swimming Australia.'

John's career leaps demonstrate powerfully that he isn't afraid of change.

'There are always opportunities being thrown up that are potentially fantastic. It is 20 per cent of people who make it happen, while 80 per cent of people watch it happen. Content people are not world champions,' he says.

'See how other people make a living. Figure out what drives you and what you are interested in, then be smart and work out if you can make a living from it. I've never met a successful person who is not passionately involved in what they do. To be successful it needs to be a 24/7 investment, not a 9 to 5.'

John also points to the importance of having mentors and being comfortable about asking for help.

'If you look at the great leaders of the world, they have typically had great mentors they've been able to bounce ideas off. I've also found that people don't ask for help very much, but in a lot of cases if they ask for help it will be provided. It's very rare for people to say no once they are approached.'

Get liberated

At this stage you may be surprised, delighted or horrified at where your career currently sits. Maybe your career isn't as healthy as you thought it was!

If you find yourself in a health zone that doesn't sit comfortably with you, then it's important to remember you can do something about it—*you can change*. In fact, you'll probably move through these different health zones at different stages in your career.

You may start your career in the liberated zone, and then over time move down to the arrogant zone as you become comfortable and complacent in your career—until, perhaps, you have no choice but to leave that comfort behind because of a restructure.

Alternatively, you may move up from the apathetic zone to the liberated zone. Different events (such as reading this book!) may trigger a change in your perspective, attitude and actions.

> Whatever zone you find yourself in now, and in the future, the good news is that you can take action to be liberated again.

When you have a liberated career, you are in control. You're in the driver's seat. You make conscious choices about which way to head, which route to take, and how and when you mean to get there. You choose how and when to leap, and that's what we'll explore next.

Start with the end

Jessica Watson OAM

In October 2009, 16-year-old Jessica Watson sailed out of Sydney Harbour with a goal. She planned to sail solo non-stop and unassisted around the world, and she had to overcome intense media criticism in order to fulfil her dream.

This adventure led to other sailing projects, authoring a book, touring internationally, producing a documentary (narrated by Sir Richard Branson, no less) and becoming the 2011 Young Australian of the Year. These days she's a partner in a startup, a public speaker and a youth representative for the UN World Food Programme, while writing her second book and studying for an MBA.

Having achieved so much at a relatively young age, Jessica has always been clear on her ambitions.

'Like any big goal, it is useful to approach a career leap by working backwards from the ultimate destination,' she says. 'It's not rocket science, but you have to start with the end in mind. That's not to say the end goal shouldn't change and evolve, but it's important to have a clear vision.'

Bringing this vision to life is about being clear on what needs to get done.

'Working on important, non-urgent tasks that support my end goal has been absolutely key. It's easy to be swept away with everyday stress, but to make that transition you have to purposefully work on the things that matter to that new role.

'Like any transition, there have been setbacks and challenges, and often things haven't happened as fast as I'd like. Navigating through others' expectations and ideas about the direction I should take has been challenging,' she adds. 'It's easy to be led down a path that isn't really where you want to go by well-meaning people around you.'

CAREER CHECKPOINT

Take five minutes to make an honest assessment:

- Are you ready to vote yourself off the island? [Yes/No]

- How likely is it that your current role will be impacted by technological change and automation? [Likely/Unlikely]

- Which career health zone are you currently positioned in? [Apathetic/Anxious/Arrogant/Liberated]

Some readers won't have answered *yes* to the first question, but many will answer *likely* to the second. Wherever you sit in the health zone, the good news is you can change and do something about it now to help you in the future.

2
REALISE
WHAT IS YOUR POTENTIAL?

'Courage and perseverance have a magical talisman, before which difficulties disappear and obstacles vanish into air.'
Former US President John Quincy Adams

In the Road Runner cartoons, Wile E. Coyote built elaborate traps to catch the speedy bird. Invariably he failed, and with a defiant *beep beep* Road Runner disappeared into the distance—until the next episode.

A few years back an unauthorised extension to the story was released in which Coyote, much to his own surprise, finally snares the Road Runner.

'Holy shit,' Coyote exclaims, 'I did it! He's under there. I got him!'

Later, when feasting on Road Runner with a friend, his friend asks, 'So what are you going to do now?'

'Never really thought about it,' Coyote replies. 'Been chasing this damn bird for 20 years. Not really trained for anything else. I guess I kind of let my life get away from me.'

We've all been in Coyote's shoes at some point or other. Doing the same thing, day in, day out. Staying in the same job because it's easier, safer, it's what we know. We may even find ourselves thinking we've been living a dream, then realising we're not! That we haven't prepared for anything else. Life has happened and we've just been along for the ride.

To focus on what you *could* do, you have to dump the preconceived notions that you or others have of you, gather your courage and fortitude, and start to dream a little about what you might *like* to do next in your career—before life gets away from you.

> ## Dump what you 'should' do, and consider what you 'could' do.

Should versus could

In the movie *Meet the Parents*, Pam's father, Jack (played by Robert De Niro), is ex-CIA, slightly nuts and highly paranoid. He has his own ideas about who his daughter should be dating, and a male nurse called Greg (played by Ben Stiller) isn't one of them.

Jack scorns Greg for his career choice, and even challenges his intellect and honesty. Greg defends his vocation, explaining why he became a nurse (even though he could have trained as a doctor) and why he finds it fulfilling. He stands his ground, despite desperately wanting to impress Jack, the father of his intended bride.

Walking away from the expectations of others isn't easy. And there are often none bigger than what career path you 'should' follow, and particularly what you 'shouldn't' do.

I've had friends who followed their fathers' footsteps by studying law—and they hated it. I've known people who became teachers because they were told 'that's what girls do'. I've had colleagues who felt enormous pressure to succeed because their parents had high-powered corporate careers. These expectations impacted the choices they made in their own careers, often negatively.

Expectations can box you in and confine your thinking, and when you are looking to leap that's not helpful. I see these pressures play out all the time when I'm working with clients going through a career transition. They experience inner turmoil as they struggle to balance what they feel they should do with what they could and want to do.

When we conform to the expectations of others, we deny ourselves the right to have the career we could have, walking away from what we really want to do.

As Sir Ken Robinson explains in his TED talk, 'Do Schools Kill Creativity?', we each need to find our true talents, regardless of where the education system seeks to have pushed us. He says, 'So you were probably steered benignly away from things at school … on the grounds that you would never get a job doing that. Is that right? Don't do music, you're not going to be a musician; don't do art, you won't be an artist. Benign advice—now, profoundly mistaken.'[11]

Such pressures carry through into our adult lives and our careers. To overcome this dilemma, we are told to find a career we love, one we are passionate about. But that often doesn't work either, and here's why.

Pop the passion bubble

One of the most popular career quotes on Google is this: 'Choose a job you love, and you will never have to work a day in your life.' This kind of claim implies that having a job you love is all roses and champagne, every day. It's not. It never is. All jobs have their good points and bad points, their highs and lows.

I love what I do, and yes I am passionate about it. But there are still times when things don't work out, when I feel frustrated and overworked. There are days when I think it would be easier back in corporate, working for someone else instead of myself. (That doesn't last for long, though!)

Passion isn't always a virtue. It can be a heart-thumping adrenaline rush driven by emotion. When you think of a passionate love affair you think of people who make short-term decisions that sometimes have long-term negative consequences.

> Chasing your 'passion' can lead you to make short-term choices that don't serve you over the long term.

My niece's experience offers a great example of this.

She was considering quitting her job. On the face of it, it was a fine job that had enormous flexibility and was a good fit with her university studies. The working environment was good too. She had a great boss and was paid well. The work didn't stimulate her though. One day she said to me, 'I'm going to quit. I'm just not passionate about the work. I need to find my passion.'

I asked her why. Well, she'd been told that she should only do a job she was truly passionate about. So I got her to write a list of all the benefits the current role offered her—in the short, medium and long term. I wanted her to think about the role in the broader context of her career. I also shared my experience of how some of the hardest (and least enjoyable) jobs I've had ended up being the ones that were critical to my future career success, as they served as stepping stones to what came next.

Through this process she was able to see that she didn't need to love the job, but the experience was going to set her up for another job that might be more in line with her interests. It also provided great contacts that would be useful for her next leap.

If she'd stayed in the passion bubble, she would have discarded a great job that ultimately helped her leap into a role she loved.

If you know what you are passionate about, that's awesome. Go you! But if you don't, that's okay too. Being told to follow your passion can also create stress, particularly if you find it hard to work out what you are passionate about. If that's you, rather than search for your passion, seek out what makes you curious.

As Elizabeth Gilbert, of *Eat Pray Love* fame, suggests, 'If you can let go of passion and instead follow your curiosity, then your curiosity might just lead you to your passion.'[12]

If you could do anything ...

'What do you want to be when you grow up?' is a question we ask children all the time. The answers we get are usually a mixture of practical reality and far-out creative thinking. A report released by the Australian Institute of Family Studies in 2017 found that six in ten 14- to 15-years-olds knew what job they wanted to chase. Of these, 60 per cent aspired to professional or managerial roles—jobs that make up only 35 per cent of the current Australian labour market.

Only 14 per cent of children in that age bracket wanted to work in areas such as retail, hospitality and administration—jobs that make up nearly half the labour market. About one in ten of the children surveyed said they wanted to be a sportsperson or entertainer or in some other way famous—the so-called fantasy occupations.[13]

The roles we aspire to as kids are rarely the ones we end up in. It's great to have dreams when you are young, and there are plenty of books and blogs out there that encourage you to follow that dream. But while I absolutely believe we are masters of our own destiny and we should dream big, as adults we also need to be grounded and practical about the future. We need to think about where jobs and opportunities will be and where they will not, about what is achievable right now and what will take some work or study on our part.

So if it's not all about chasing your passion or childhood fantasies, where do you start? You start with purpose.

Swallow the purpose pill

If you're not familiar with Simon Sinek's TED talk on the golden circle and how good organisations have a clear 'why', then I suggest you Google it and watch it sometime soon.

Sinek explains that organisations typically know 'what' their mission is and 'what' products or services they're selling. They also know 'how' they develop and sell a product or service. What is often missing is the 'why'. And yet people, or customers, don't buy *what* you do; they buy *why* you do it—they buy in to your purpose.

It is the same with your career. Your why (your purpose—the reason for your what and how) should be at the centre of your career decision making. Your why is followed by the how (your technical and behavioural skills, values and competencies) and what (your profession—the output you deliver or the service you provide), as shown in figure 2.1 (overleaf).

By putting your why at the centre of your decision making, you consider your career choices as part of your whole life, taking account of your family, friends and colleagues, health and happiness, community and societal needs, personal and lifestyle goals, and spiritual fulfilment.

Figure 2.1: start with why

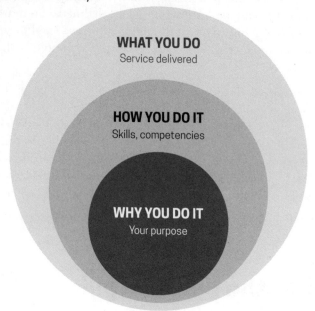

Finding your purpose or why isn't simple. There's no magic formula and you won't find it just sitting around. It is an iterative process involving a fair bit of soul searching and paying attention to what matters to you and motivates you. For some people it involves study, experimentation and pushing the boundaries of what's possible. For others the focus is on helping others, creating a better community or building a sustainable future.

In the context of your career, your purpose may be to find a job/career that helps you create a happy, healthy family life or enables you to explore the world and learn more about yourself and others. You may want a job/career where you keep learning, get to help make the world a better place or help people develop fulfilling careers. Alternatively, it may be that you simply want a job/career that offers you autonomy and flexibility so you can pursue a life outside work.

Your why can also change at different stages in your life and career. In my early career, my why revolved around material success and status. I only discovered my real why (a deeper why) when I set up my own business later on.

When you know your purpose, why you are doing what you want to do, then you gain the confidence to take charge and be in control of the decisions that count. It also helps you overcome any obstacles you face along the way, as you're spurred on and motivated to keep going when times are tough.

The following exercise encourages you to take some time to think about your why by considering what really matters to you.

Exercise 2.1: Figure out your why

Thinking about your purpose or motivation, write down words, thoughts and ideas over a period of a few days. You may be someone who likes sketching ideas or creating Pinterest boards — whatever works for you. The object is to capture your ideas, feelings, emotions, moods and impressions. The ideas don't need to be perfectly formed, so long as they have meaning and resonance for you.

This is the start of your thinking about what 'could' be in the context of what matters to you, whether it involves family, friends, health, spiritual contentment, community service, personal goals or career achievements.

These ideas will percolate, bubble up and eventually spill over. When that happens you will know you have hit on something. It will feel right, and you will feel good when you think about it.

Know why

Clare Payne

Clare Payne began her career as a solicitor for a big city law firm. Then she moved to work in-house for an investment bank, where she leapt internally to focus on ethics. Over time she moved out on her own, working as an independent ethics adviser across a range of industry sectors.

Throughout her career, Clare has always been clear on why and how the work she does aligns with her interests and values.

'There's always a common thread,' she explains. 'I focus on informed decision making and I work to create a good and just society.

'I believe individuals should follow their passions and interests and seek an alignment between their personal values and professional life. If a career leap could bring someone closer to this alignment, then I think it is the right thing to do.'

Her career leaps have been well thought out. She always discusses her plans with other people and seeks advice in advance.

'The most challenging aspect has been not having a clear picture of what the future will look like. Instead I've had to focus on the present, which isn't such a bad thing, as really none of us can be certain about the future.'

Find your rhythm of life

If you're a bit stuck on finding your purpose, then the next exercise will help. You will ask yourself, are you where you want to be in terms of your life? Are you dancing to your own rhythm or is your life off beat in some way?

Once you have identified whether or not your rhythm is working as you'd like it to, you can begin to identify the elements of your life you may want to shift as you consider your career leap.

Exercise 2.2: Find your rhythm of life

1. Every week has 168 hours. Fill in the table with estimates of how much of that time you spend each week on:

   - **career** — work and activities associated with your job and developing your career

   - **connections** — caring for others, socialising, spending time with the people who matter to you such as friends, family and colleagues

   - **finance** — organising and managing your financial goals

   - **learning** — reading, learning and practising new ideas and skills, and participating in courses

   - **lifestyle** — leisure pursuits and things you do in your 'down time'

- **self-care** — sleep, exercise, meditation and other activities that contribute to your health and wellbeing

- **service** — giving back to others through such activities as community service and volunteering.

Activity type	Percentage of time allocated each week	Satisfaction level
Career		
Connections		
Finance		
Learning		
Lifestyle		
Self-care		
Service		

2. Now ask yourself honestly (without judgement or self-justification) whether the time allocated to each activity makes you feel:

- satisfied

- dissatisfied

- unsure/ambivalent.

3. Do a quick self-assessment (again, without judging yourself). What does this exercise tell you about how you currently prioritise your time?

Look at what you spend a lot of your time on and derive satisfaction from, as well as where you are dissatisfied with the amount of time you are spending. Then note where you would like to spend more or less time.

As you reflect on these insights, consider their potential significance for your future career choices. For example, if you are currently spending disproportionate time each week working, leaving little or

(continued)

Exercise 2.2: Find your rhythm of life (*cont'd*)

no time for your family, perhaps you need to seek a career option that offers more flexibility. If the time you are currently devoting to learning is very limited, perhaps you want to pursue a career path where you will be able to spend more time learning. If you are dissatisfied with the time you have to spend in service to the community, perhaps you should seek a new career direction that will provide that opportunity.

What's holding you back?

Victoria Beckham once said she wanted to be more famous than Persil Automatic, a laundry detergent that is a household name in the UK. When she entered the music scene in the early 1990s as part of the Spice Girls many people (me included) wrongly assumed that Posh Spice and the group would be a 'one-hit wonder'. Fast forward 25 years, and she's a successful and respected fashion designer. She ignored her critics, aimed high — and got there.

Much of what happens in life is based on what we tell ourselves and how we interpret both internal and external commentary.

Our internal commentary is frequently shaped by what other people say or think about us. And yet those opinions are just that — opinions. We need not necessarily accept them as facts.

ASK YOURSELF

- What beliefs do I have about my career and where I'm at now?

- What views do I hold about my ability to make a career leap or to do the thing I really want to do?

- What beliefs are holding me back or are no longer relevant?

- Which of those have been imposed on me by someone else?

- What new beliefs do I need to create to help me leap?

What do you tell yourself about your career and your ability to leap? Do you think it's impossible or more than possible? Are your thoughts helping or hindering you?

To leap, you need to ditch the expectations of others and any limiting old beliefs, put yourself securely in the driver's seat and willingly set off into an uncertain future.

Get in the driver's seat

You don't want to be a passenger in a future hurtling past you, nor do you want to be a backseat driver with no control or to be stuck on cruise control or autopilot. You want to be the one who makes decisions about which direction to travel in, how fast to go, any detours to take and the support crew you need to get you there. That's the only way you'll ever end up at your chosen destination.

Once in the driver's seat you move from being in a dangerous place in your career, where you are threatened with market obsolescence, towards a future in which you have a competitive advantage, as illustrated in figure 2.2.

Figure 2.2: on autopilot or in the driver's seat

ON AUTOPILOT	IN THE DRIVER'S SEAT
FIXED MINDSET	GROWTH MINDSET
DEFAULT THINKER	INTENTIONAL THINKER
SUBMITTED ACTIONS	COURAGEOUS ACTIONS
MARKET OBSOLESCENCE	COMPETITIVE ADVANTAGE

Let's look at what it takes to climb into the driver's seat in your career.

Growth mindset

Your mindset plays an enormous role in determining the success of your career. It is an important part of who you are, shaping your attitude, thought processes, decisions and behaviour.

As unique individuals, our mindset is shaped by our personal experiences. We interpret the world we live in and what is happening based on our beliefs, perceptions and assumptions. It is this interpretation that drives our internal state, and ultimately our emotions, thoughts and behaviour.

The danger is that our mindset can limit us, and we may not be consciously aware of this.

It can set up roadblocks and obstacles that make it much harder to achieve our career objectives. Worse, it can lead us down a path where our 'faulty thinking' creates 'faulty choice' and ultimately delivers a 'faulty outcome'.

A quick way to check your mindset is to ask yourself the following question: 'Do I believe (1) that I know everything I need to know already or (2) that there is still much to learn?' How you answer this question will help you determine if you have a *fixed mindset* or a *growth mindset*.

These terms were coined by Stanford academic Carol Dweck. She found that people with a fixed mindset see intelligence as static, 'a fixed trait'. As a result, they always like to appear smart, as though they have all the answers. They believe that success is based on talent alone, not work. This means they will avoid challenges and give up more easily. They also ignore feedback, which they see as criticism, and they feel threatened by the success of others.

This mindset will put constraints on your career, because over time you will stop learning and stop taking risks, both of which are prerequisites for growth and development. A fixed mindset stalls your career progress.

In contrast, people with a growth mindset believe that intelligence can be developed through hard work and effort. Consequently, they are eager to embrace learning, take on new challenges and persist in the face of setbacks. They love learning and usually display higher resilience. They are also more willing to learn from others and receive feedback.

A person with a growth mindset cultivates learning at every opportunity. They recognise there are always different and better ways to approach an issue. Such a mindset helps you nurture a sustainable career. You are better able to cope when things don't go your way—for example, when a job application or interview goes badly.

Cultivating a growth mindset is critical when you're trying to leap and change careers.

Exercise 2.3: Check your mindset

Assess where your mindset currently sits using this checklist, and see where you could make some improvements and move towards a growth mindset. Which of these elements would you tick off as applying to you?

Fixed mindset	Growth mindset
I feel threatened by other people's career success.	I draw inspiration from other people's career success.
I ignore feedback on my work, dismissing it as irrelevant.	I welcome feedback and seek to learn from it to advance my capability and career.
I give up easily when I get knocked back, and I avoid challenges.	I persist with my career goals, despite challenges and setbacks.
I'm convinced I'll never get any better at that task/work, so there's no point in trying.	I constantly look for ways to improve my work and my life.
I hear myself saying:	I hear myself saying:
'I'm no good at this.'	'What else can I do? What might be missing?'
'This is good enough.'	
'I give up. I can't do this.'	'I'm proud of my work effort. It's good work.'
'This is as good as it gets. I can't do any better.'	'With practice and effort, I'll be able to do this.'
	'I can always improve my work.'

Intentional thinker

We all have default ways of thinking and patterns of behaviour. These subconscious thought processes and actions often play out as habits — the things we do because we've always done them. They feel safe, comfortable and familiar.

When you are doing something new, looking to make a leap, you need to break the old habits and patterns of default thinking and embrace intentional thinking. When you are intentional, you are *considered* (you have weighed up the pros and cons of your ideas) and *deliberate* (you are aware of your decision making and take accountability for it).

We make decisions every day: what to wear, what time to go to work, how to answer an email. We also make decisions with our career: what role we apply for, whether to stay or go, to do more study, to apply for that promotion.

These decisions involve choices. By deciding to do one thing over another, we make an intentional selection from a range of options.

Good choices, particularly when it comes to your career, are considered.

It takes effort to make a considered decision, in which you weigh up the pros and cons and think about what you may need to 'trade' as a result. Remember, when you deliberately decide to do one thing it often means you are choosing to forgo something else.

It is much easier to avoid making the decision or to ask someone else to make the decision for you. However, avoiding a decision is still making a decision; you've just decided not to take action yourself!

It's also easier to make decisions on impulse based on your current emotional needs or what you feel like doing here and now, with little regard to the long-term consequences.

Consider your decision-making habits: How do you usually make decisions? Do you avoid them? Are you impulsive or deliberate? How does your current mode of thinking negatively impact your career choices? How could a different mode of thinking positively enhance your career choices?

You may need to disrupt or discard your decision-making habits in order to become an intentional thinker who makes considered and deliberate career decisions.

Courageous actions

In her best-selling book *Yes Please*, Amy Poehler recounts how one time, when she was on an overnight train to New York, she was rudely awoken by someone who dumped a script on her lap as he was disembarking. Clearly he had the expectation (or perhaps hope) that she would read it and help him leap into stardom.

Needless to say, she didn't help him. She was incensed by his assumption that he could achieve his goal so easily—by getting someone else to do the hard work for him.

As Poehler puts it, 'Good or bad, the reality is most people become "famous" or get "great jobs" after a very, very long tenure shovelling shit and not because they handed their script to someone on the street … People don't want to hear about the fifteen years of waiting tables …'[14]

Now you may be thinking, 'Hey, give him 10 points for effort. At least he asked the question—isn't that being courageous?' Courage would have been staying on the train and waiting until Amy had woken up before approaching and speaking to her. He might have had to miss a meeting or be late for an appointment, but he would have seized the opportunity to have a direct and respectful conversation with her, rather than being intrusive and discourteous while selfishly hoping for the best.

Courage is being willing to do the hard work to change both ourselves and our circumstances when we need to, rather than submitting and accepting that change is outside our control. This may mean taking a hard look at ourselves and working out what in us needs to change, so we are ready for the future that we want to be a part of.

Erik Erikson's theory of human development has shown how our personality, temperament, capabilities and development aren't fixed. We can change them if we choose to. According to his eight-stage theory, between infancy and old age we all face a series of development challenges. How we respond to those challenges either derails us or enables us to forge ahead, yet the outcome at any stage isn't permanent and can be modified by later experiences.

At the fifth stage of development, during adolescence, we face an 'identity crisis' during which our identity is challenged by a sense of role confusion. Our identity gives us a clear sense of who we are and our values and ideals. Identity or role confusion arises when we fail to develop a 'coherent and enduring sense of self', and so have 'difficulty committing to roles, values, people or occupational choices'.[15]

Our identity is shaped, in large part, by the work we do.

Our sense of who we are — our identity — doesn't become fixed at adolescence but continues to evolve. Much of our identity is attached to the work we do, our occupation, even the title we have. So when our role or career changes, so too does our sense of identity. Which is exactly what Herminia Ibarra found.

An economist and professor of organisational behaviour, Ibarra discovered that a fixed view of our professional identity can hold us back. She refers to this as 'authenticity paradox'. In her research on people going through a leadership transition, she found that a career advance requires us to move outside our comfort zone while resisting a strong impulse to protect our identity.

Ibarra found that in new environments, such as a new workplace, we can be unsure of ourselves, worrying about whether we will match up to the expectations and perform well. It is in these types of situations that we can fall back into old, more familiar ways of behaviour that make us feel comfortable. Ibarra suggests that it is more helpful if we view ourselves as 'works in progress', whereby we evolve 'our professional identities through trial and error'. By taking this approach we are able to develop a style that fits — suiting us and the organisation's needs.[16]

That's why when someone loses their job they often feel like they've lost a big chunk of their identity, so they don't want to tell people — they keep it hidden. Conversely, when a person moves up the hierarchical ranks, their sense of status gets a boost, and usually so too does their image of themselves.

To make a leap, you need to be willing to change how you see yourself, to have the courage to move towards a new identity. (We work on shaping your identity in chapter 6.)

Be a star-shaped peg

Nigel Matthews

Nigel Matthews is something of a leap expert. He began his work life as a glazier, then he trained as a counsellor before working as a salesperson, gymnastics coach, business owner and business consultant. He is currently a finance executive in the asset management space, managing around 25 000 assets valued at more than $1 billion. Not bad for someone who finished school in year 10!

Nigel refers to himself as a 'star-shaped peg in a square hole'. School didn't stimulate him, but that didn't hold back his quest for knowledge and growth. He currently has three postgraduate degrees and is resisting the temptation to take on another. 'I love learning and always have, which is why I think I have leapt so much,' he explains.

However, he believes his broad career experience has been more valuable than any degree. 'You are only limited by what you put your mind to. Sounds like a cliché, but it's the truth,' he says.

'Recruiters and employers are very quick to make judgements. When I narrowed my field of view—where I was leaping from and to—and differentiated between what I thought I could do and what others thought I would do well, then my messaging about why I wanted to transition and how my skills were transferable made sense to everyone.

'Convincing yourself that your skills are transferable and that you are ready for what lies ahead of you is the first thing,' he says. 'But you also have to convince your partner, family, recruiters, employers and peers.'

Are you willing to leap?

We all have personal circumstances that can impact our willingness and ability to make a leap. These can involve personal commitments, our financial position and lifestyle expectations. It's important to understand how willing you are to shift these parameters in your pursuit of a different career.

Your circumstances will influence how flexible you are with your career—whether you are, for example, able to move to another location or need flexible working arrangements. Having young children, or kids in school, may limit your willingness to relocate. You may be saving for a house or paying off a mortgage and therefore require a certain level of regular income. You may have a really strong drive to achieve and make your mark in the world. You may have very few commitments that tie you down and be obsessed with learning and want to take off and explore the world. Or you may have particular preferences about the type of work you do and the industry you want to work in.

Being clear on your circumstances provides practical parameters that will help to shape your career leap choices.

Exercise 2.4 will get you thinking about some of these realities. Remember, there are no right or wrong answers. You just need to be honest and realistic about what it takes to leap and what's possible for you personally.

Exercise 2.4: Audit your personal circumstances

In this exercise you'll reflect on the context of your career change, personal commitments, financial position and lifestyle expectations.

1. Purpose and context

Consider the context of your career leap, and if the shift is optional or obligatory — and therefore how quickly you are seeking to leap. Your change may be driven, for example, by a desire to do something different or by your role being eliminated or changed due to AI and automation.

Write down the reasons for your career leap. Reflect on the work you did earlier in the chapter on your why and purpose. What does this tell you about what is important to you in undertaking a career leap?

2. Role requirements

Identify the specific job requirements that need to be considered when planning your career leap. This may include your preference for full time or part time, contract or permanent, one role or a portfolio of roles, or being self-employed or a salaried employee.

If you want to be a salaried employee, consider also: your desired job level, whether or not you want to manage people, your preferred work environment, and whether there are industries you won't work in or organisations you don't want to work for.

If you want to run your own business, identify any specific considerations that need to be factored into your decision. This might include the type of business and service offering, and the experience, planning and funds required to establish it.

Are you able to work anywhere or are you geographically bound? You may need to eliminate jobs where relocation or frequent travel is required, or you may be seeking a job where you can work flexibly — from home, anywhere in the world or with a compressed working schedule.

3. Financial position

Dig into your financial position to determine whether it facilitates or potentially constrains your leap.

First, calculate the minimum income required to support your current lifestyle as well as the desired target level. Then identify other necessary benefits such as an ability to access extended holiday leave, sick leave and study support, and to participate in incentive schemes or receive other benefits not related to salary.

Next, examine your current expenses and consider if there are areas where you might reduce spending to fund your leap. Remember, you may need to make short-term sacrifices to achieve your ultimate career leap goal.

Look at the amount of money you have in reserve and how long this would last (based on your expenses) if you didn't earn an income for a period of time. This will tell you whether you can realistically exit your current employment before you secure a new role, and how quickly you will need to land your leap.

4. Lifestyle expectations

You need to get real about the energy, risk, time and money you are willing to devote to making your leap. If you think this is going to be effortless, sorry — think again!

Ask yourself:

- How much effort am I willing to put into learning new things to facilitate my leap? [None/A little/A lot]

(continued)

> ## Exercise 2.4: Audit your personal circumstances (*cont'd*)
>
> - Am I willing to pay for new learning (or other resources) that may be necessary for my career leap? [Yes/No/Maybe]
>
> - How willing am I to take a risk with my career by trying new things and venturing into new areas? [Low/Medium/High]
>
> - How willing am I to sacrifice leisure time to devote time to making my leap happen? [Low/Medium/High]
>
> Take a moment to look at what you have written for each of these sections. What does it tell you about the key elements that need to be considered as you select your career leap destination? Are there parameters that are likely to constrain your ability to leap? If so, can you change them?

F—k you money

I've worked with lots of people during my career. What distinguished those who were truly content with their job was that they didn't feel trapped by it. They had a sense of freedom, and more often than not that freedom came from having money in the bank.

Money doesn't buy happiness, but it does buy freedom.

Financial freedom doesn't mean you are a multimillionaire; it means you have enough money in the bank that you are not tied to one location, one job, one occupation. Freedom gives you power when you negotiate. It gives you options when you leap.

This money in the bank is what I commonly call 'f—k you' money. It gives you wiggle room and the comfort of knowing you are not tied to a job. It's likely not enough to retire on, but it's enough to provide at least three to six months of reserve in the bank if you want to walk away or if something happens in your life.

Everyone's circumstances are unique. Many people struggle to make ends meet, but lots of people spend money on inessentials, and this choice can limit their career options. Having a cash reserve is about making conscious choices. Enjoy the occasional treat, but not at the expense of your long-term financial security and career freedom.

Having money in the bank enables you to push the envelope on things that matter to you. It makes the decision to leap easier and far less stressful. It also means you have the funds to support you while you are preparing to leap.

When you are looking to leap, you need to be honest about your financial position. If you have massive financial commitments or debts, then you need to be confident that your new destination will provide enough to pay the bills. If you have no cash reserve, you can't leave your current place of employment until you have your next gig lined up. Consequently, your choice of where and when to leap may be more limited. You need to think ahead.

CAREER CHECKPOINT

Congratulations! You have completed phase 1.

Before we move on, let's check your progress:

- What expectations do you have of yourself or do others have of you that may be holding you back?

- What's your purpose, the why in your career?

- Is your mindset ready to support your leap?

- Are you willing to decide intentionally?

- Will you take courageous action when you need to?

- Are you aware of your personal circumstances and what you may need to change in order to make a leap?

PHASE 2
ARCHITECT
Where do you want to be?

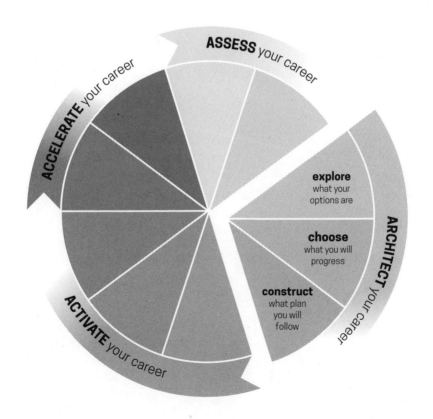

ASSESS your career

ACCELERATE your career

explore
what your
options are

choose
what you will
progress

ARCHITECT your career

construct
what plan
you will
follow

ACTIVATE your career

You're still here—great! This means you have made an intentional decision to take a different path ahead. Now you are ready to explore, experiment and investigate your career leap possibilities.

In phase 2 you'll learn what style of career you have and how this can help you leap. You will critically examine your industry and transferable strengths, and start to map some possible career options, however big or small your leap may be.

This is your opportunity to deliberately construct and design the career you want based on your personal goals, priorities and circumstances. This phase will show you *how*.

3
EXPLORE
WHAT ARE YOUR OPTIONS?

'The only true wisdom is knowing you know nothing.'
Plato

In 1984 Dr Barry Marshall, a physician from Perth, Australia, drank a cocktail of bacteria to prove a point. Before his research project, carried out with pathologist Robin Warren, conventional thinking was that peptic ulcers were caused by stress and poor eating habits, so treatment advice was limited to taking antacids and modifying one's lifestyle. As Dr Marshall put it, 'To gastroenterologists, the concept of a germ causing ulcers was like saying that the Earth is flat.'[17]

Within only a few days of drinking the *Helicobacter pylori* bug, Marshall began getting symptoms, and it wasn't long before a biopsy showed the bacteria had colonised his stomach. In a nutshell, he had proved to the scientific community, and indeed the world, that it was this type of bacteria, not lifestyle or food choice, that caused peptic ulcers.

At the time, Marshall and Warren were working with lots of unknowns and against what everyone else thought. They pushed boundaries, unfazed that their peers thought their research was a complete waste of time. The result? In 2005 the pair were awarded the Nobel Prize in Physiology or Medicine, one of the highest awards to which a scientist can aspire. It put their careers firmly on the world map.

Leaping in your career takes guts and determination. You have to be willing to explore new ideas, challenge the norm, experiment with what's possible and take risks (though perhaps not ones that might directly affect your health).

How far are you willing to explore and experiment in your career?

Navigator, Surveyor or Pioneer?

In marketing, consumers are categorised, according to how willing they are to embrace risk, as innovators, early adopters, part of the majority crowd or laggards.

A similar concept applies to when you leap. Individuals have different comfort levels when it comes to changing their career and choosing the path they want to follow. As shown in figure 3.1, you are likely to have one of three career styles—Navigator, Surveyor or Pioneer—depending on your tolerance, or indeed enthusiasm, for taking a risk, experimenting and stretching yourself with your career options.

Figure 3.1: your career style

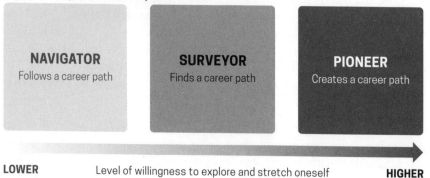

| **NAVIGATOR** | **SURVEYOR** | **PIONEER** |
| Follows a career path | Finds a career path | Creates a career path |

LOWER   Level of willingness to explore and stretch oneself   HIGHER

Everyone is different, so understanding which style best suits you will help you determine what are feasible and realistic career options. It's important to remember that none of these career styles is in itself 'bad' or 'wrong'. It's all about how far you're prepared to stretch yourself and leap in one go.

Let's look at each career style now.

Navigator

If you are a Navigator, you like to know precisely the steps you need to follow to land a role. You want to understand where you're going and exactly how you're going to get there. You prefer to follow a well-trodden path, an easily understood route laid out before you that shows a clear progression. With a compass and a map in hand, you're more comfortable pushing forward.

As a Navigator, you have a low risk profile and appetite for career change. You prefer to take the safe, well-tested route in your career and are reluctant to experiment with the unknown (no drinking from petri dishes for you!).

You need to look for career leap options that are still quite closely related to your current role. Think small steps first. For example, you might leap from one functional area to another within your company.

Surveyor

Do you constantly seek new ideas and knowledge? Do you tend to get bored easily? You are probably a Surveyor. You like to stretch your mind and your capabilities. You are pretty comfortable with change and view risk, exploration and experimentation as a necessary part of your career.

This means you are willing to push the boundaries and take the less established or well-trodden routes in your career. You are always keen to discover new roles or options that you may not have considered before.

You see a number of options when it comes to leaping in your career. Potential destinations could become stepping stones to somewhere else more exciting. For example, you might leap from working in a corporate role to leveraging that knowledge as an external consultant providing services in your current field of expertise, before making another leap to running your own consulting firm.

Pioneer

Do you like to explore career options few people have attempted? Then you are probably a Pioneer. You are inspired by a love of creating something from scratch. You are not concerned that there is no clear path ahead. It's that challenge, that risk of the unknown, that spurs you on.

You love experimenting with ideas and outcomes, unrestricted by rules and structure, and can often appear unconventional in your career choices (something your friends likely comment on). This means your options are boundless! You could leap from being an architect to a radio announcer; a dancer to a lawyer; a plumber to an inventor; a banker to a business owner. It's important, however, to remember to have some grounding on which choice you will make and when. You'll need some constraints to narrow down your many options.

Where are you now?

It's important to remember that your career style isn't fixed. As your life circumstances change, so too can your willingness to experiment and push the boundaries with your career leap.

You may begin as a Pioneer, then, midway through your career, you may choose to step back to a Navigator style as you take on different responsibilities in your life. Later still, you may progress to being a Surveyor and then a Pioneer again.

So spending some time thinking about where you are now will help you determine where you're going to leap to. Are you drawn to a career that has low risk and where the path forward is clear and relatively certain? (Then you are likely a Navigator.) Do you favour a career where there is plenty of challenge and opportunity for learning, as well as some unknowns and uncertainty? (Then you are likely a Surveyor.) Do you prefer a career with loads of experimentation and unknowns, and with no clear path ahead? (You are surely a Pioneer!)

Now consider: How has this style helped your career to date? Has it hindered your career development in any way? If so, how? What might you need to do differently to make a successful career leap this time? Perhaps you need to increase your comfort level, be more willing to experiment, explore and take a risk to make your desired leap.

Where could you be?

Now you have a grasp of how willing you are to stretch yourself, you can use this understanding to help you work out some leaps you might make. You can leap across functional roles, occupations, industries, levels, organisations and geographic zones, or any combination of these. The more elements involved, the more effort and stretch that is required for you to make the leap.

Let's have a look at how this works in practice using an example.

If you are moving from a role in finance to one in risk and staying in the same organisation, you are only moving functional roles and so the level of stretch required is low, matching with the Navigator career style.

If, however, you are making the same functional role change, but also changing organisations and industries, say moving from financial services to mining, then the level of stretch is higher. This is more likely to match the Surveyor career style.

At the other extreme, if you are moving away from finance to working as a TV presenter, then the level of stretch is higher again, more matching the Pioneer career style.

In exercise 3.1 you are going to compare your stretch level (how far you might be willing to leap) with your current career style.

Exercise 3.1: How far are you willing to leap?

How you approach this exercise will depend on whether you already have some career leap ideas or not. If you have a number of potential career leap ideas already in your mind, write them down. For each of those ideas, determine how many of the career change elements would be activated by a leap of that type. If you don't yet have career leap ideas, then look at each of the career change elements and consider which you are likely to want to change as part of your career leap.

(continued)

Exercise 3.1: How far are you willing to leap? (cont'd)

The table below shows combinations of the career change elements and the likely level of stretch involved, then suggests the career style most suited to a leap of that nature. If you'd like to see more examples, you'll find details in the online resources available for this book.

Career change elements						Level of stretch	Career style
Functional role	Occupation	Industry	Organisation	Level	Country		
✓						Low	Navigator
	✓					Low	Navigator
✓					✓	Medium	Surveyor
	✓	✓	✓			Medium	Surveyor
	✓	✓	✓	✓	✓	High	Pioneer
✓	✓	✓	✓	✓		High	Pioneer

Using the table as a guide, determine the level of stretch involved from each identified career leap option and see if it matches the career style you identified earlier. If it doesn't match, consider what might need to change: think about either changing the type of leap or adopting a different career style.

Remember, if you are a Navigator, you are more likely to prefer a lower level of stretch; if a Surveyor, a medium to higher level of stretch; and if a Pioneer, you will typically seek the highest level of stretch possible.

Don't be a dodo

When exploring your options, be aware of what is changing around you. For example, you need to keep abreast of what's happening in your industry, so you are prepared for any changes that may impact your role and profession. You also want to leap to a viable destination.

There's no point leaping into a role that's about to go the way of the dodo.

The best way to understand what's happening right now, and what will happen in the future, is to research it. Get online and find relevant articles. Talk with colleagues and associates, and people in your current or desired industry or professional association. Ask what is changing, and where they see gaps and opportunities. Chat with people you know who work in the role, industry or profession you're considering to build a realistic appreciation of how feasible your transition idea is.

Technology will disrupt you in some way, whether it's positive or negative. Some roles will become redundant, while others that are process oriented will be given to a machine, and new roles will be created. According to a 2017 report from the McKinsey Global Institute, those of us in caring, technology or knowledge roles will be the least impacted, while technicians, processors and people doing predictable physical work will be most impacted, as shown in figure 3.2.

Figure 3.2: technology's impact on occupations

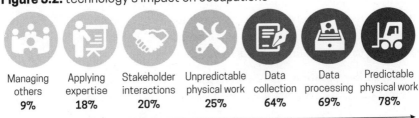

Managing others	Applying expertise	Stakeholder interactions	Unpredictable physical work	Data collection	Data processing	Predictable physical work
9%	18%	20%	25%	64%	69%	78%

Technical feasibility: % of time spent on activities that can be automated by adapting currently demonstrated technology

0   50   100

Data source: McKinsey Global Institute report, 2017[18]

Many professional 'knowledge workers', such as software engineers, lawyers, pharmacists, accountants and consultants, have yet to be massively impacted by technology change. In their book *Only Humans Need Apply*, Thomas Davenport and Julia Kirby suggest a knowledge worker's job is under threat from automation if:

- automated systems can do some of the role's core tasks

- it involves little physical contact or manipulation with the client/customer

- it involves simple content transmission or the creation of data-intensive content

- it involves straightforward content analysis and answering questions that are data dependent

- the tasks can be simulated in some way or performed virtually

- there are rules or defined parameters that specify how the work is done.[19]

Taking this a step further, PwC's Anand Rao suggests there are three ways to categorise AI and its impact on organisations: *Assisted intelligence* improves what the organisation is already doing; *augmented intelligence* enables organisations and people to do things they couldn't do without the help of the machine; and *autonomous intelligence* creates and deploys machines that act on their own.[20]

This means that as organisations grapple with how they use AI, they are ultimately making decisions based on determining (1) what human tasks can be automated, (2) what tasks can a computer do that a human can't, and (3) what tasks can a human do that a computer can't.

Where an organisation finds the return on investment from introducing automation stacks up, then it will be goodbye human job.

The upside is higher value tasks that require more than a computer can provide will be in great demand — creating new career options for us all.

We can expect to see a wide range of new work roles in years to come. In the medical field, for example, futurists are making predictions about the new area of nanomedicine, in which specialist 'nanomedics' will work at a molecular level, using tiny robots to investigate and treat disease and physical conditions. There may also be memory augmentation surgeons, who help restore memory in people with dementia and Alzheimer's.[21]

At the same time, roles that currently exist will be expanded. For example, as the level of freelancing increases there will be a greater need for personal brand coaches and professional tribers — freelance professional managers who specialise in bringing teams together.[22] There will continue to be a need for people with cyber-security, application development and technology skills, and for specialists in the caring professions.

Automation of repetitive and mundane tasks will free more of us to follow creative pursuits that computers can't do, as well as roles that require social and emotional competencies, such as caring for others, providing expertise and coaching, and leading and developing others. Such key skills, and social and emotional capabilities, will remain essential and highly valued into the future.

Skills matter, but competencies matter more

Competencies are abilities, attributes or behaviours that are necessary in order to be highly effective in a role. They are often referred to as 'soft skills' and include, for example, reasoning, creativity, problem solving, judgement, common sense, compassion and empathy.

Unlike technical or professional skills, which are often job specific, competencies are generally applicable across a range of jobs. For example, some (not all) of the competencies for a human resources manager would be equally useful for a finance manager. Some of the competencies for a teacher are similar to those required of a change manager or a learning and development professional.

The competencies that are in demand by employers or the employment market change over time. So it's useful to compare the competencies considered essential now with those likely to be most in demand in the future. A report published by the World Economic Forum predicts the 10 competencies that will be most in demand in 2020 will be: complex problem solving, critical thinking, creativity, people management, coordinating with others, emotional intelligence, judgement and decision making, service orientation, negotiation and cognitive flexibility.[23]

These sought-after skills and attributes are transferable across many roles and industries. Your competencies will help you identify your options and land your leap.

You are not Usain Bolt (sorry!)

Remember the last time you watched, or saw a commercial for, *Who's Got Talent* or *The X Factor*? It's often painful watching those contestants with delusions of grandeur but without the talent to support them. Unfortunately, many of us have a warped perception of our capability. We sometimes fail to self-reflect honestly and to critically examine where we may need more skills and competencies.

It's important to accept that we all have limitations. There are some things you will be great at and some things you won't. No matter how hard you try, train or put in your 10 000 hours, it's not likely you will beat Usain Bolt in a sprint (I certainly wouldn't!). You need to realistically identify your strengths and the areas needing ongoing improvement and development.

> When you leap you need to know how to play to your strengths.

It is easier to choose and make that leap when you play to your current strengths. It is these strengths, these skills and competencies, that will help you stand out as you transition across roles or industries, or whatever your leap involves. You will use these strengths as a launching pad for your career leap, highlighting them in your LinkedIn profile and when talking to prospective employers or clients. They are critical building blocks for success in your new career.

So let's get real about your strengths — what you have, what you don't have yet (but could acquire through learning and practice), and what you won't ever have. In exercise 3.2 you will rate yourself on your level of proficiency (from *1 = no skill* through to *4 = expert*).

When thinking about your strengths, what first springs to mind? Do you think about your technical or professional skills such as in project management, social media, data analytics, maintenance, operations, training or quality assurance? Do you think about your occupation, for example defining yourself as a doctor, accountant, carpenter, bricklayer, technician or IT programmer? Or do you think about your competencies such as your verbal, reasoning and creative abilities, and what you are naturally good at?

As you do exercise 3.2 you will want to think about your strengths from all those angles.

Exercise 3.2: Rate your strengths

Looking at your technical/professional skills, your current competencies and the in-demand competencies, self-rate your level of proficiency, using the scale:

1. No current skill/competency
2. Some skill/competency, but not proficient
3. Proficient at the skill/competency
4. Expert with a high degree of skill/competency.

(a) Technical/professional skills

Using your CV and past roles as a guide, list all the technical and professional skills you have, self-rating your level of proficiency.

(b) Current competencies

Rate yourself against the competencies relevant to your current profession. If you need help, Google your occupation and the word 'competencies' for a relevant list.

(c) Future in-demand competencies

Rate yourself against the competencies that are likely to be in most demand in the future:

complex problem solving	emotional intelligence
critical thinking	judgement and decision making
creativity	service orientation
people management	negotiation
coordinating with others	cognitive flexibility

What strengths can you take with you?

The obvious answer to this question is all of them! But some will be more important than others, depending on where you are leaping to.

That doesn't mean you won't want to learn more. There will be attributes you will want to expand and strengthen as you leap. There will also be attributes you will need to acquire.

If you are lacking in a skill that might help you leap, then you may need to do more work on acquiring it. This will take time and may influence whether you want to leap to that destination (we will look at this in the next chapter). If you want to become a lawyer, but it's going to take you five years to get a law degree, then you may want to set your sights on leaping somewhere else first!

In exercise 3.3 we return to your strengths to identify which are *transferable* (directly applicable in another industry or occupation), *adaptable* (usable in another industry or occupation once they have been modified in some way) or *replaceable* (likely to be industry or occupation specific, and therefore not as useful when leaping to another career).

Exercise 3.3: Pinpoint your versatile strengths

Using the strengths that you identified in exercise 3.2, consider whether they are transferable, adaptable or replaceable. This will help you pinpoint the versatility of your strengths.

YOUR STRENGTHS (technical/professional and competencies)	For each category answer yes, no or maybe		
	Transferable	Adaptable	Replaceable

Turn up the heat

You have now determined your career style and have a sense of how far you are willing to leap. You've examined how your industry is changing and considered the longer-term viability of potential career destinations. You've also looked at your strengths to see what might be helpful when you leap into your next career.

Curiosity is critical at this juncture. It's by being curious that your mind expands to embrace ideas. One technique to help you generate possible career options is *hothousing*, which is used in idea generation for product or strategy development.

When you hothouse you write down lots and lots of ideas—even if, on the surface, some may seem implausible or impractical. If you want to have even more fun with this, look at a role that appears to be the polar opposite role to the job you are currently doing. *The New York Times* has even created an online tool (Google 'What is your opposite job?') to help you do so.

Using US Labor Department records on the skills and tasks required for each job, that site looks at the skills that a job uses most and least, and compares them to the skills needed and not needed for other roles. For example, the opposite job of a pharmacist is a model. Why? Because a pharmacist uses skills such as chemistry and information processing, whereas a model needs to maintain physical balance and coordinate body movements—not priorities for a pharmacist.

In exercise 3.4 (overleaf) you are going to hothouse your future career ideas based on the strengths you identified earlier and push your thinking a step further outside the box. Remember, it is your strengths (in particular those that are transferable) that will help you leap, so it helps to start with your strengths and expand from there.

Don't rush! Spend some time on this activity, but not so long that you get stuck and don't move forward. You may want to talk to people around you whom you trust. Source ideas from those who work in different areas or fields, or even in roles you have never contemplated.

Exercise 3.4: Hothouse your career leap options

Imagine:

- What if you took a job that paid 50 per cent less but that you loved 50 per cent more? What could that role look like?

- What if you re-engineered your current job? What could that involve?

- What is the biggest career leap you could possibly take?

- What would be an unexpected leap, one you haven't considered before?

- What role have you always wanted to take on but never acted on?

- What if you take on a role completely different from what you are now doing? What might it be?

- If you could write your own job description, what would it look like?

- If you worked for yourself, what would you do?

- When you look at your strengths and consider what you love doing, what comes to mind?

Get real

By now, you've got a list of ideas, some better formed than others. You may even know exactly where you want to go next. That's great.

Whatever position you are in, it's important you take a healthy reality check on what that career, those options, look like and feel like in practice. You want to uncover what you are likely to be doing each day if you work in that field or role.

The only way to do this is through research and asking lots of questions of people who are actually in the role or operating in a similar field. What do they love? What do they find boring? What parts of their job drives them nuts, or gives them satisfaction? What are the good and not so good points with work of this nature? If they could change any aspects of their work, what would these be? What do they wish they had known before they started down this track? Which companies or organisations are leaders in this industry? Are there any educational barriers to entry?

Ask as many questions as you need to really get a feel for what it might be like to do that work. These conversations are essential, and particularly useful if you're thinking about going out on your own, whether freelancing or starting a business.

It can be easy to fall into the trap of viewing a new role or career through rose-tinted glasses, then ending up bitterly disappointed when the reality doesn't match up to your dream.

Critically assess your list of options and see if there is anything you'd like to take off the list or change in some way before you move on.

A surprise destination

Rodney George

After 20 years in senior financial roles, including as chief financial officer, Rodney George took a career leap in a quite different direction.

When he resigned from his corporate job he initially thought he'd seek another role in the finance space, but as it turned out he landed as a retail travel consultant.

'It is scary, daunting. You can feel like you have failed in your career or life,' he says of his leap. 'It took me about two months to announce the change in my career publicly. But I have learned that if you have skills and are smart you can start over. There will be some pain, but you can re-establish yourself.'

Making this shift involved a significant readjustment, not just in terms of salary and lifestyle, but in relation to his position in the organisational hierarchy.

'I was moving to the bottom of the corporate ladder in terms of seniority. I was very much used to being the leader, making decisions, issuing instructions, leading change, influencing organisational behaviour. Now I was a little cog again.

'It took me about three months to settle into the role and find it in myself to say, "I am going to make a go of this." Once I had some wins, I started to believe I could do it. I also started to gain respect from my colleagues and managers, who saw more potential in me. From there I was able to progress once more in terms of promotions and achievements. This made it easier to sleep at night.'

Rodney emphasises the importance of having the right people around you to support you when you make this decision. 'You are already so worried about the decision yourself that you do not need naysayers around you.'

And what would he do differently next time? 'I now know that I can do it and that different people will come to value my skills and experience. It really is about getting your confidence back and reclaiming your sense of self-worth.'

CAREER CHECKPOINT

In this chapter you've explored the style of career you have now, how willing you are to stretch and leap, and how the world of work is changing.

You've now identified a number of career possibilities that you can refine as you move on to the next stage of the Career Reinvention Cycle.

Before you do, let's check your progress:

- Are you clear on your career style, and whether it is helping or hindering your career progress?

- Have you got an understanding of how far you are willing to leap?

- Do you understand how your current and desired industry and occupation are changing?

- Have you outlined your strengths?

- Do you know which of those strengths are replaceable, adaptable and transferable?

- Have you pushed your thinking and explored ideas around where you could leap to?

- For these options, have you checked in and researched what it might be like to work in that space?

4
CHOOSE
WHAT WILL YOU
PROGRESS?

'The way out is through the door. Why is it that no one will use this method?'
Confucius

In Lewis Carroll's *Alice's Adventures in Wonderland*, Alice follows the White Rabbit and falls down a rabbit hole. She has no idea where she is and embarks on a series of adventures.

At one point, she meets the Cheshire Cat in the woods and enquires:

'Would you tell me, please, which way I ought to go from here?'

'That depends a good deal on where you want to get to,' said the Cat.

'I don't much care where—' said Alice.

'Then it doesn't matter which way you go,' said the Cat.

'—so long as I get SOMEWHERE,' Alice added as an explanation.

'Oh, you're sure to do that,' said the Cat, 'if you only walk long enough.'

In your career, you certainly want to get somewhere, and you should very much care where that somewhere is. You want to be clear that your somewhere isn't leading you just anywhere.

By now you may have a fairly precise idea of the leap you want to make. You may have decided to leap from your current career to becoming a doctor, financial commentator, media personality, landscape gardener or interior designer.

Alternatively, your destination may be less clear and your 'somewhere' may be no more than a couple of options on the table that you want to explore further. Perhaps you love creating things, and are tossing up between becoming an architect or an app developer. Or perhaps you love helping people, and you're thinking about working as a professional life coach or as a carer for the elderly. It may be that you are thinking about stepping up in your current company or changing departments.

If your idea is still a bit fuzzy that's perfectly okay. If you are tossing up between two or three possible leaps, this next stage will help you narrow down those options.

To leap successfully, you need be able to clearly articulate to the market what you want to do, otherwise people won't know how to help you. You'll just come across as confused and uncertain. You won't be able to direct your energy productively. You'll waste a lot of time 'tinkering' around the edges, rather than focusing and directing your time and effort.

> Clarity is important, because without a sense of direction it will be very hard to make a career leap.

Find the sweet spot

Too much choice can be overwhelming and lead to procrastination, indecision and inertia, none of which is helpful when you are wanting to make a leap!

As Barry Schwartz explains in his TED talk 'The Paradox of Choice', having too many options to choose between doesn't make us feel better off. Marketers, in particular, have operated on the belief that it's better to offer consumers plenty of options so they are more likely to find what they want. It turns out that this may be a myth.

Schwartz argues that instead we need to find the 'sweet spot', the point at which we benefit from variety, while not being paralysed by it. 'Choice is good,' he says, 'but there can be too much of a good thing.'[24]

Be warned, however. In the attempt to filter and find your sweet spot you can also kill off a good idea just because you're worried or fearful about making the leap. You want to filter, but not by fear or because of other people's expectations.

Be mindful if you hear yourself saying, 'Yes, but …', 'I've tried this before …', 'I don't have time …' or 'This is too hard …' Or if others say to you: 'What do you know about that?', 'So many people who do that fail—it's too risky …', 'Wow, that's hard!', 'How can you afford to do this?', 'That's fine in theory, but in reality it's a pipe dream …' or 'Don't you think someone else has already thought of this?'

When it comes to your career, the best way to filter is to get practical and draw some boundaries around your possibilities. This is about filtering out ideas that won't fit with the practical realities of your life and your vision of the life you want to lead.

To get clear, to get direction, the question to ask yourself is:

What are you willing to trade?

You can't have it all

You will never get everything you want in life. That's a fact. Sometimes life doesn't go according to plan, but this doesn't mean your life can't be well lived. I love my life, but that doesn't mean I have everything I've always wanted. I couldn't have children. I'd love to be a few inches taller and to have skinnier legs. I could go on …

It's the same with your career. Choosing to take one direction means you are choosing not to do something else. A career choice you make usually means giving up other things. These tradeoffs come in all shapes and sizes.

One of my clients walked away from a large corporate role because he wanted to work part time. This enabled his partner to step up to a bigger role, while he could spend more time with the children. Another client decided to walk away from the security of a 9 to 5 job in favour of a totally different industry that she loved. Another traded a successful role with the fat pay cheque for more time and space to do other activities.

Personally, my career motivation has always centred on a love of learning and being challenged. However, in the past I have also valued financial security. When I walked away from a corporate role, I traded the security of a defined income for something that mattered more to me at that point in my life—autonomy. The freedom to choose how I worked, where I worked, and who I worked with.

To make these tradeoffs you need to know, for example, whether the role's location is more or less important to you than money. You need to know whether you are willing to forgo leisure time on the weekend to learn a new skill that will help you land your career leap. You need to be clear on whether the status of the role is more important than having a role that's flexible.

> The clearer you are on what you are willing to trade, the easier it is to identify the career destination that best meets your needs.

Decisions, decisions

When companies develop strategies they usually establish decision criteria to help them assess and compare the various options on the table. Then they can objectively look at the options and determine which one best fits with where the organisation wants to go.

We are going to take a similar approach now.

You have three career decision criteria to consider: *career specifications* (including workplace environment, salary, status and alignment with your life goals); *level of risk* (and your willingness to make the leap given the risk involved); and *level of effort* (and your confidence in being able to make the leap in your required time frame).

Career specifications

Think of your career as a product with specifications. These include salary and work benefits; title and status; and work environment (including flexibility, ability to work autonomously, and the organisation's culture). There are also intrinsic benefits, such as the sense of achievement you derive from what you do and alignment with your life goals.

In exercise 4.1 you will order and match your specifications.

Exercise 4.1: Assess your career specifications

In table 1, rate the most important specification number 1, the second-most important number 2 and so on (include additional specs if you need to).

Table 1: order your career specifications

Career specifications	Order of priority
Alignment with life goals	
Autonomy	
Learning and challenge	
Money/financial security	
Status/power	
Sense of achievement	
Work environment and flexibility	
Other:	
Other:	

Looking at your prioritised list, select your top three and list them in table 2. Then add in the career options you identified in chapter 3 (using as many columns as necessary), and compare each option to your top three specifications to see if they are met. Answer yes or no.

Table 2: Match your career specifications

Priority career specification: Is this spec met? Yes/No	Career option 1	Career option 2	Career option 3	Career option 4
1				
2				
3				
Career matching				
Does this option match your top three priority career specs? Yes/No				

Level of risk

Many things we do in life that are worthwhile have an element of risk associated with them. There are always risks associated with a career move, because what you're doing is inherently uncertain. But that is not a reason NOT to do it!

The risk of doing *nothing* is that you stay in a role that makes you unhappy or is about to become obsolete, or, worse, you don't get the opportunity to really make the difference in the world you were born to make.

The risk of doing *something* is that your leap may not land well. But if that happens you just go and do something else or go back to your original field. Remember, the upside risk is also that your leap lands well and turns out to be an awesome career move!

What's the risk of doing nothing versus the risk of doing something?

In exercise 4.2, you'll examine the potential risks attached to your career options. Just as some leaps require more effort, some leaps carry more risk. Risks can be grouped into four types:

1. **Financial**. You may earn less during the transition to your new career. If the leap doesn't work out, you may have a period when you are not earning an income or not earning enough to cover your expenses.

2. **Health/stress**. A career change can be stressful on you and on those around you, especially if the leap isn't going well or is taking longer than expected.

3. **Relationships**. If your leap isn't supported by the significant other in your life, making a career change can put a strain on your relationship.

4. **Reputation**. Your reputation and market positioning can be damaged if the leap isn't managed well.

You may also have other risks particular to your circumstances. If so, note them down.

Exercise 4.2: Assess the level of risk

For each career option, assess the relative risk for each risk type — rating either low, medium or high. Once you've done that, look at the total level of risk for each leap option, considering which option has the least risk and the most risk, and what level of risk feels acceptable for you. You want to make a decision as to whether or not you are willing to take on that risk.

Risk categories: What is the level of risk involved? Low/Medium/High	Career option 1	Career option 2	Career option 3	Career option 4
Financial				
Health/stress				
Relationships				
Reputation				
Other:				
Cumulative level of risk				
Is this level of risk acceptable to you? Yes / No				

Level of effort

Now look at how quickly you need to land your leap. You may have no time frame, or a set time frame in which you need to change careers or land a new job. At the same time, look at the effort required to land your leap.

Your required time frame and the effort involved need to match up. For example, if you have to land a new job quickly so you can afford to pay the rent or the mortgage, but it is going to take a long time to get to your desired destination, then it may not be a wise move (yet).

ASK YOURSELF

- How far do I want to leap? (For example, across functional roles, occupations or industries — the further the leap, the greater the stretch required. Typically, the greater the stretch, the more effort required.)

- What volume, type and complexity of new skills, knowledge and competencies do I need to acquire to leap and land well? (The more that are needed, and the greater their complexity, the more effort you'll need to put in.)

- Do I need to establish new networks, or will the leap involve broadening or deepening existing networks? (If you need completely new networks, then once again a greater level of effort is required.)

- How much repositioning will I need to do in the market to establish myself in this new career? (The more repositioning you have to do, the greater the effort you'll need to apply.)

- What other activities may be required to make the leap happen?

While the leap may score very high on effort, that doesn't necessarily mean it isn't worth pursuing. It's about being aware of the effort you are willing to invest and being realistic about the time frame in which you need to make it happen.

Bear in mind the words of the philosopher and author Alain de Botton: 'There is no such thing as a work–life balance. Everything worth fighting for unbalances your life.'[25]

Exercise 4.3: Match your time frame with the effort required

Use this exercise to help you assess the level of effort required for each potential career leap option. Note whether the effort is low, medium or high (relative to the other options). Then decide if the effort involved matches the time frame in which you need to make the leap.

Typically, the greater the level of effort, the longer it will take to leap; and the lower the level of effort, the shorter time it will take to leap.

Effort assessment: How much effort will you need to put into the following activities? Low/Medium/High	Career option 1	Career option 2	Career option 3	Career option 4
Level of stretch				
Skill acquisition				
Networks being established				
Market repositioning				
Other activities				
Cumulative leap effort				
Does the effort match the desired time frame in which you need to leap? Yes/No				

Own your fears

Layne Beachley AO

Layne Beachley AO is a seven-time world surfing champion (six of them consecutive), making her the most successful female surfer ever! But her career didn't end when she retired from surfing.

She now runs her own charitable foundation, Aim for the Stars, and is Chair of Surfing Australia. She is also an author and a highly sought after professional speaker and trainer on sustaining success, overcoming challenges and maintaining a winning mindset.

Her biggest piece of advice: 'Take the leap.'

'Tim Ferriss often speaks about negativity bias, which is exaggerating the riskiness of certain moves and underestimating the opportunities of others,' she explains. 'If we only focus on the cost of moving from the known to the unknown we will never take the leap. So ask yourself, "What are my fears?" and own them. You can't change what you can't see.'

This doesn't mean you won't have doubts.

'As an athlete I had the utmost belief in my ability, but when it came to taking the stage as a speaker I initially doubted myself and questioned my ability and the relevance of my message. Doubt and anxiety are all part of uncertainty, which is directly linked to fear.

'Action is the antidote to fear,' she adds. 'So keep putting one foot in front of the other and remember, distractions and disappointment are detours, not dead ends.'

Layne says sharing her fears with others who had taken leaps before her, asking for advice and reaching out to experts and leaders in similar fields, all helped.

'I received a formal written complaint after the first motivational talk I ever gave, so I had to improve if I was going to make it in the competitive market of motivational speakers,' she says. 'I'm still fine-tuning my presentation—and feedback is my friend.'

Sink or swim?

What you've just done is very logical, and sometimes logic can land you in the wrong spot—especially if you haven't listened to how you feel through this process. As you look back over the exercises you've just done, what do you notice?

ASK YOURSELF

- Is there an option that stands out as worth pursuing?

- If so, which is it and why?

- How does the thought of pursuing that career option make me feel?

- If there is no clear option, do I need to adjust any of the ratings?

- What is my gut reaction to what I'm seeing?

- Is there an option that matches my career specifications, yet I am uncomfortable with the level of effort and risk? If so, what might need to change?

If you experience a sinking feeling or a sense of dread as you say to yourself, 'Oh, that's not what I want the answer to be', then ask yourself why. Maybe you haven't answered the questions in a way that really resonates with you, or you haven't stretched yourself enough to discover what it is you really want to pursue. If that's the case, take some time to reflect on this before you go on.

You need to be at the point where the direction you're heading in feels natural. It feels good. That doesn't mean you are free of doubt or uncertainty. Remember, career leaps into the future are risky, and they require effort. But you will feel that you are about to leap in a new direction, and that it is the right thing to do.

The next step in your journey requires formulating a plan to get there.

Don't wait for the duck
Anna Jenkins

Anna Jenkins has leapt many times in her career—from medical research to occupational health and safety to human resources, and she's now working for one of Australia's largest regulators. Her leaps have taken her across industries and from full- to part-time work.

She has learned that it takes hard work and planning, but you can't wait until all your ducks are lined up. If you do, she warns, 'You could be waiting forever before you leap. Don't wait until you've devised the perfect plan, as it is unlikely to ever line up like that.'

But it's not just about the big leaps, it's also about getting lots of experience, exposure and opportunities in the job you are in, as these become the building blocks for your next leap.

Anna's advice: 'Stop comparing yourself to everyone else. Run your own race.' At the same time, 'Be generous with your time and expertise to others in your profession or workplace. If nothing else, it makes you feel good.'

You also need to stay connected to what is happening in your industry, your company, your profession. 'If you take your eye off what's going on, you won't be able to take advantage of the opportunities that are actually presented to you, while you are dreaming of the ones you want.'

CAREER CHECKPOINT

Filtering your career leap options is a big step forward.

Before we move on from this stage, let's check in:

- What are you willing to trade to make your leap happen?

- What are your top three career specifications, and which career leap option best meets them?

- What level of risk is involved in the options you are considering, and what are you willing to take on?

- How much effort is required for each of the options?

- Does the effort required match the time frame in which you need to leap?

- What choice have you made about your career leap destination?

- Do you feel comfortable with the direction you're heading in and, if not, what do you intend to do about it?

5
CONSTRUCT
WHAT PLAN WILL YOU FOLLOW?

'Take the course opposite to custom and you will almost always do well.'
Jean-Jacques Rousseau

Many years ago I heard Steven Bradbury speak. An Olympic speed skater, he famously won a gold medal at the 2002 Winter Olympics because everyone he was competing against in the final had fallen over. It was literally a case of 'last man standing'. The media attributed his overnight success to 'luck'. What they failed to report on was the years of planning, sacrifice and hard work that had brought him to that point.

Success doesn't come easily to anyone. It involves thorough planning and determination.

Just how will you make your leap? Will you stay in your current role a bit longer while you prepare for the change, or will you suddenly up and leave? Many people stay in their current job until they have landed a new career, devoting their spare time to helping them land. Others quit and focus all their efforts on getting to the next destination. There's no right or wrong. It's a matter of weighing up the pros and cons and then constructing your plan.

Do you want a side with your main?

Some people do what's called a 'side gig', 'side hustle' or 'moonlighting', effectively following what I call the 'dual track' approach to leaping. This means staying in their current role and starting work on their leap at the same time.

For example, a former colleague of mine was a communications consultant for a large company, while on the side she ran a social media company that provided local support for celebrities when they were in Australia.

Taking this approach is a great way to try out your new destination and see how you like it. You can test the parameters, build the infrastructure and contacts, and transition over a time frame that works for you.

It also provides a safety net as you have guaranteed income coming in from one source, while you are building up an income stream from another source. Over time you can wean yourself off the first as the second one picks up. If the second one doesn't grow as planned, you still have the security of the original job. Alternatively, you may decide you want to keep a foot in both your old and your new world, maintaining your 'dual track' for an indefinite period.

On the downside, using the 'dual track' approach means you may feel like you're holding down two jobs for a period of time. You need to think about how long you can sustain it for, and at what point you may want to fully leap to your new destination.

> The advantage is you can dip your toe in the water; the disadvantage is you may feel burnt out. Weigh up the pros and cons.

If you're going to adopt this approach, you need to make sure all your work that relates to your second gig is done using your own equipment and technology. Keep a separate laptop, mobile phone and all the infrastructure you need to set yourself up. Do not use your company's or organisation's property.

Many organisations frown on this kind of activity, and you could find yourself in a sticky situation if you don't handle it correctly. Read your employment contract carefully, including the small print you might normally ignore. You may need written consent from your employer to get involved in outside work. I needed to do this when I joined a not-for-profit board while working in financial services.

It's likely you won't be able to use any information you gain from your current work environment to help your new venture; that may be viewed as a conflict of interest and akin to stealing, so is not a good look for your résumé or profile. It's also likely your employment contract will include an intellectual property clause, which means anything you create while working for the company belongs to the company.

There are plenty of legal precedents on what happens to employees who flout this law. Getting sued by your former employer isn't a great way to start your career leap!

In some arenas this is changing as companies acknowledge the benefits of nurturing talent and recognise that they will lose valuable people if they don't permit some flexibility.

Do you tell your boss?

I once worked with a person who knew, before he left corporate, that he was going to set up a consulting firm. So he used every spare minute he had to get ready. He set up his brand, website, value proposition, infrastructure—everything he needed to make the leap. He did this while working full time and keeping his work commitments ticking along, and his boss knew about it. In fact, once he left the company his former boss hired him to do consulting work.

But it doesn't always play out like that. Whether or not you tell your boss you are planning on leaving will obviously depend on the type of relationship you have with them and whether you think they'll support you or try to sabotage your efforts.

They may be suspicious of your activity, wondering what you are doing on company time. If there's any potential for a conflict of interest or any concern that your new work might compete—even in a small way—with what you do currently, then be very careful about what you say and do. Quite often in sales, investment banking and areas involving proprietary knowledge employees are given their marching orders as soon as they accept a position with a competitor or decide to go out on their own.

There is no right or wrong here. You've got to use your intuition, and your understanding of the relationship and work context, and be realistic about what could happen. It may help to seek advice from a trusted adviser or colleague who knows your work environment.

All or nothing

Your other option is to leave your current job before you have landed your leap. Some people will see this as risky: 'Why would you throw in a good job when you have no certainty of your next destination?'

Well, nothing is certain these days in the world of careers—you know that! Like it or not, changing careers involves a level of risk. This is about assessing your own level of comfort with risk, an assessment you made in the previous chapter.

Then again, some people argue that it's much easier to get another job while you are still in a job, but that simply isn't true. If you're not tied down to a job, then you have the flexibility to start whenever you need to (no notice required). This can be a big advantage if an organisation needs help pronto.

If you decide to quit work to devote yourself full time to your leap, then you will have ample time to focus on landing well. Without the safety net of a current job, your drive to make the leap happen increases. There's nothing more motivating than the need to earn money to pay the rent or mortgage. Be careful, however, not to put yourself in a situation where you'll make hasty choices or silly mistakes because of this pressure.

This is where your 'f—k you money' from chapter 2 comes into play.

Remember, it's a great idea to have a cash reserve to sustain you while you are in transition mode.

Why stop at one?
Aneka Manners

Aneka Manners isn't your typical banking executive. She's also a fashion designer, business owner and artist, and a perfect example of how your career can lead you down dual tracks.

'Don't assume it's a binary argument,' she says. 'Simultaneous careers are the "new black".'

This doesn't mean her transition has been easy—far from it. There were 'a number of nights spent in the foetal position, crying, self-medicating or procrastinating, then realising I was procrastinating,' she admits.

'I would not be here doing what I'm doing today without two years of hard, introspective work with two coaches.

'I'd got to a point where I knew something was standing in the way of my true fulfilment but I couldn't nail what it was ... Great job, great husband, great stepchildren and family—why am I not yet fulfilled? Why the despair? What first-world problem is this?

'I asked for help and decided I was willing to let go of some limiting beliefs and be generally terrified in exchange for getting my life back, along with a simultaneous career.

'Turns out, when you're not following your path, it bites you in the arse (eventually) and you have to take action,' she explains. 'My path was what I had already chosen as a child but had left behind—fashion, art, creativity.'

Here, in a nutshell, are Aneka's biggest learnings for those deliberating on making that leap:

- You won't lose what you think you will (and that includes the things you're most scared of losing).

- The drama in your head is just your old self trying to protect you from what it can't see—say thanks and move on.

- No one is coming to give you permission or approval. It's not because they don't wish you well, but because everyone has their own stuff and frankly they're busy with it. Stop waiting and get on with it.

- You will find support and friendship in the strangest places, and if nothing else ever happens, that discovery will be enough and be transformative in a different way.

Give it life

Now you have decided on your destination, you've got to make it real, to make it visible to you and to others. This is the only way you will commit to moving forward.

It is helpful to write your desired destination as a statement—for example:

- I am going to have a career as a designer.

- I am going to be a teacher, focusing on children with special needs.

- I am going to build a technology startup.

- I am going to start a business where I build new capabilities.

- I am going to be head of marketing for a global company based in Hong Kong.

- I am going to keep my current job and start an online digital agency on the side.

It might seem inconsequential, but getting your career leap out of your head and committing it to paper or your digital device cements your decision and will help motivate every step you take from this point on.

Put a target on it too, a date to work towards, and explain why this leap is important to you. Use your work from chapter 2 on your *why* to help you with this.

For example:

I am going to be working as an interior designer by November 2018, leaving my current role as a financial adviser behind by June this year. This will fulfil my creative interests and provide the flexibility, career satisfaction and income I need.

This is how you breathe life into your idea, turning it from dream to reality.

Leaps aren't accidents
Steve Bracks AC

'A leap doesn't happen by accident; it's largely by design,' says former Premier of Victoria, the Honourable Steve Bracks—and he should know.

He started working as a secondary school teacher across private, state and Catholic schools. He went on to become a municipal recreation officer in the local council and the executive officer of a Commonwealth community education centre, before moving from Ballarat in central Victoria to Melbourne for a role in the public sector. All the while he was building the foundations for his parliamentary career.

'I had a career and life planner, which I carried in my wallet,' he explains. 'It mapped out that my ambition was to be in Parliament before I was 40 years of age. If I didn't achieve that ambition, the plan was to go into the public sector with the aim of becoming a head of department. I got pre-selection for the seat of Williamstown at the age of 39.

'In my career plan, I had mapped out where I wanted my parliamentary career to go, and I actually achieved what I wanted one election earlier than I had originally planned,' he says.

Steve Bracks served three terms as premier of Victoria, after which he moved into advisory and board work.

'You have to be prepared — to do the groundwork, as well as keep your options open. It takes significant preparation and planning. You have to know what you want and have a plan in place to achieve it.

'So while I had an existing career as a secondary school teacher and then in other areas, at the same time I was actively involved in the local community. I was doing a lot of voluntary work and building contacts and skills in the areas necessary for me to enter politics. Then when an opportunity arose to run for pre-selection, I was prepared for it.

'I always had the ambition to be in state or federal parliament, which meant that throughout my career I was doing things to build the groundwork for that — for example, running the student union, getting involved in environmental campaigns, in local campaigns, actively engaging with the community. This was all in addition to the professional work I was doing.

'When the opportunity came up for me to step into public life, all the groundwork had been put in place.

'It's always a little scary, when you enter public life, as there is no safety net for a politician,' he says. 'You're at the whim of the public and party mood. The party selects you, then every three years the public determines whether you deserve the right to continue. If you want to move into more senior positions in politics, you also need to get the support of your colleagues.

'This means you have to be prepared to take a risk. You're walking away from a steady professional career, and there's no fallback position. You have to really want it, to be single-minded and confident in your own ability.

'There will be difficulties along the way. There will be setbacks, so don't be put off or be deterred. You need to be resilient, to make sure you play the long game and don't give up at the first sign of turbulence.'

Knowledge is power

When it comes to planning your leap, knowledge is certainly an advantage. Your leap will happen because of who you know and what you know.

Every career leap involves some form of learning. What will differ is the amount, nature and complexity of the learning, and whether it is optional or mandatory.

This knowledge may take the form of qualifications, certifications or technical skills that must be gained before you can move into a field. For example, fitness instructors need certification before they are licensed to practise. Doctors need a medical degree. Psychologists need a degree and industry practice. Teachers need an education degree. Plumbers need to have completed an apprenticeship and to be licensed.

In other fields no formal qualification is mandatory, but job experience is highly valued—think TV presenter, radio announcer, graphic designer or social media expert. Consider whether formal qualification or on-the-job experience is more highly valued for the leap you want to make.

Some learning may need to be completed before you leap, while other steps can be taken during or after you leap. When I was moving from an advisory role to the head of compliance of a large financial institution, I made the leap before I got my certification as a compliance professional. Having that qualification wasn't a prerequisite for the job, but I knew that it would give me an edge once in the role.

Identify your knowledge gaps then work out how to close those gaps and set your timeline for doing so (exercise 5.1 will help you with this). Remember, it may not involve a lengthy university degree. It could include reading books, enrolling in courses, subscribing to journals or online news feeds, meeting new people and perfecting new practices.

Websites such as edX, Coursera, Udemy and Open2Study offer free or low-cost courses across a range of subjects. Perhaps you need to investigate a short course to brush up on your industry or computer skills.

Some people love learning, while others find it a chore and find the idea of setting aside time to close their learning gaps challenging. If that's you, just remind yourself of how much this leap means to you, and why you want to do it. As the Chinese proverb goes, 'Learning is a treasure that accompanies its owner everywhere.'

Gaining knowledge is, like your leap, an investment that pays off tenfold in the end. There will be times when you need to open your wallet and put down some cash for a qualification, a book or a journal, or the services of a coach. This is an investment in your future. Leaping, like any kind of success, doesn't come for free.

The more you are willing to invest in learning, the easier it will be to make a career leap.

Let's start by determining any knowledge gaps you may have, and then work out how to close those gaps and set your timeline for doing so.

Exercise 5.1: Plan your learning acquisition program

Use this exercise to specify your learning gaps, what you need to do about them and the timeline involved. It's also useful to note whether the learning is optional or mandatory.

Learning gap	Optional or mandatory	Steps to close	Due date
Technical skills required for the destination			
General and specific knowledge required for the destination			
Competencies required for the destination			

Never stop learning

Dr Lisa O'Brien

Most of us imagine that medical professionals follow a linear career path. But Dr Lisa O'Brien leapt from medical practitioner to medical administrator, to health services consultant, to a role in an IT startup, to CEO of Australia's largest education charity for disadvantaged children.

At each point in the journey, Lisa acquired new skills and qualifications, including in medical administration, along with a Master of Business Administration and a Master of Human Resource Management and Coaching. She also leapt from full- to part-time work while she was raising her family.

'Working part time can be difficult in senior line management roles,' she admits. 'The combination of my MBA and my experience gave me the opportunity to work in new settings, including consulting in health services planning, in an IT startup venture and in a biotech commercialisation. My desire to work in part-time roles influenced my choices to some extent; however, each role provided me with a broader base of experience and allowed me to develop particular skills.'

It was during this time that Lisa worked pro bono to help establish Lou's Place, a drop-in centre for homeless women. This experience sparked her passion for working in the community services sector.

'Ultimately, being offered the opportunity to become CEO of The Smith Family was a dream for me. The role drew together all the threads of my life to that point—my various skills and experience, my interest in social justice and equality, and my pragmatic desire to make a difference. Now, some six years later, I'm delighted to say I still love it!

'Those who have skills and knowledge that are transferable to multiple sectors will fare better.

'Making a career leap is a real positive, but to do it well you need to be proactive about looking for opportunities and to not limit your growth and potential. Flexibility in thinking is key, remembering that every job is an opportunity to grow.

'When I started my career I certainly didn't have a clear perspective on my capabilities and characteristics as a leader. That self-awareness grew over time through the successive challenges that I dealt with.

'I also learned not to lock myself onto a single career path. There are lots of good reasons for taking a sideways step, whether it is to take on caring responsibilities, for health reasons or to change career direction,' she says. 'There can be hidden potential in this lateral move. And who knows, it may be the one that propels you towards your ultimate career passion. Keep an open mind, be courageous and embrace the new!'

Be a master planner

A plan isn't a definitive playbook that maps out every eventuality or a precise route with all the GPS coordinates. It is a general guide that helps you execute your career leap.

It sketches out where you are going, how you are going to get there, what you need to get done and by when. Without it you'll spin your wheels, procrastinate, waste time — and stress out about how hard it is to leap. You'll likely end up nowhere.

But your plan can't be too rigid. You need flexibility, as the path may deviate as your unknowns become knowns.

Aside from learning, there will be other gaps to close or actions to take to make your leap happen and to execute it well. Consider the following areas:

- **Finances.** Ascertain what you need to do to ensure your financial position is secure enough to support and facilitate your leap. Perhaps you'll want to talk to a financial planner or your bank, start a regular savings plan, or cut back on other living expenses so you can build up a cash reserve to fund your leap.

- **Infrastructure.** Research and purchase all the equipment you need to enable your career leap. This may include a new laptop, mobile phone, premises, or specific supplies and stock.

- **Knowledge base.** Determine a specific set of actions to build your knowledge base on the market you are entering so you are equipped with the latest insights. This may require your joining an industry association or subscribing to relevant industry news alerts.

- **Legal.** Understand what's required in terms of legal frameworks, insurance, taxation, business registration and compliance with relevant laws and regulations. Where necessary, seek independent legal advice to ensure you don't get burned later.

- **Market positioning.** You will need to do lots of work to understand your current and future market positioning. You'll also have to update your profile on LinkedIn and other social media platforms to build your brand and reputation in your new market. We'll do more of this in the next phase.

- **Network.** Spend time determining who you know, who you need to know and how you plan to meet them, and how to deepen your network to help secure your leap. You will spend time analysing and planning this in chapter 7.

- **Other activities.** Are there other activities specific to your career leap? If so, what are they? Map out those details.

Set dates against each of your activities. Dates drive action and provide markers to monitor to keep you on track. With no 'due dates', it becomes too easy to put tasks off for another day.

Spend some time completing exercise 5.2. When you look at what you have written down, ask yourself, 'What don't I know about this career option that I should know?' and 'Who [or what] can help me fill in those blanks?' Factor your answers into your plan.

Exercise 5.2: Prepare your master plan

Fill in this table with the details of the specific activities you need to do to make your career leap happen. This will form your master plan!

Activity type	Your specific actions	Due date
Finances		
Infrastructure		
Knowledge base		
Legal		
Market positioning		
Network		
Other activities		

Mind map it

If you don't like this linear planning approach, try a mind map. A mind map is a visual way of organising information and ideas.

At the centre of the map, write your career leap destination, then connect to that all the primary activities you need to undertake to make your leap take off and land well.

For example, each of the primary activity types listed in exercise 5.2 would branch out from the middle of your mind map. Each of those primary activities would then have a number of associated activities and tasks, forming sub-branches, and so on.

I used this technique when I started my consulting practice. Sure, I had a more detailed business plan as well, but it was my mind map that I pinned to my office wall. This visual representation of my plan gave me a daily reminder of what I needed to do.

Whichever planning approach you adopt, your plan won't be perfect at this point. It's a beginning, and you will keep building on it as you go through the Career Reinvention Cycle.

Target and track

Set up markers so you can track and assess your progress. Your targets might include, for example, the number of new people you have met and talked with each week, and the amount of time you've spent working on making your leap happen. They might also include the number of tasks in your plan that you have completed, whether you are on or off track with this, and the amount of research on your new career/industry you've done.

These targets are for the activities that help you progress towards your career leap goal. The targets you select will depend on your particular plan, so identify ones that are meaningful in the context of your leap.

Most importantly, keep your plan visible to remind you of what you need to do, and of how much progress you are making towards your leap.

Plan not perfect

Dr Bronwyn King

Witnessing firsthand the devastating impact that smoking has on a person's health eventually set Dr Bronwyn King, a radiation oncologist, on a path towards a career leap she says is still 'in flight'.

During a meeting with a representative of her superannuation fund she discovered that some of her contribution was flowing to tobacco companies via her fund's default option. Having watched hundreds of people die from tobacco-related diseases, this wasn't a good fit for her.

Bronwyn approached her super fund, and after numerous meetings and a presentation to the board she convinced the organisation to go tobacco-free. This was a pivotal step towards establishing the Tobacco Free Portfolios organisation, which she now leads. It works across the globe to inform, prioritise and advance tobacco-free investment by eliminating tobacco from investment portfolios.

As her career in this space has expanded, her work as a radiation oncologist has compressed.

'The leap happened organically and I am in fact still leaping, somewhere in mid flight, and not exactly sure where I am going to land,' she explains. 'From the first step I had to learn to be comfortable with uncertainty.

'Early on, many of my colleagues and seniors were quite bemused, some even openly critical of my even considering doing less oncology to make room for Tobacco Free Portfolios. One person who backed me right from the start was Professor David Ball, one of the world's foremost lung cancer specialists.

'On the day that the first superannuation fund announced they were going tobacco-free he sent me an email saying, "By this action you will save more lives than in an entire lifetime as a clinician." That was all I needed to keep going. If Professor Ball thought it was a good idea, then I knew it was worth pursuing.

'To me, there was more risk in doing nothing. If I had done nothing I would have regretted it forever,' she says. 'I had a chance to make a difference and I wanted to at least try.'

Bronwyn insists you don't need to have all the plans in place before you start.

'I often reflect on a comment from a friend of mine, when I mentioned to her that I didn't know where I was going. She said, "Just keep stepping forwards. The path is forming under your feet." It was brilliant advice. It really captures the sentiment of risk and uncertainty, but also the sense that it is going to be okay.'

CAREER CHECKPOINT

Well done on reaching the end of phase 2. While you've made some great progress in planning your escape, there is still a lot more work to be done.

Before moving on, check your progress:

- Have you outlined your career leap in as much detail as possible?

- Have you identified the learning required to support your career leap, and created a program to close any required learning gaps?

- Have you built a high-level plan (with dates) that maps out the key steps in your career leap?

- Have you identified how you will target and track your progress so you can see how you are travelling?

PHASE 3
ACTIVATE
How will you get there?

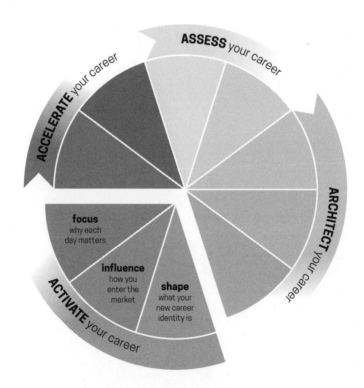

ASSESS your career

ACCELERATE your career

ARCHITECT your career

ACTIVATE your career

focus
why each
day matters

influence
how you
enter the
market

shape
what your
new career
identity is

In this phase, you'll shape your career identity to best position yourself for your new career. You'll assess how you see yourself and how others see you. You'll review and establish your online presence, and consider how to ensure your first impression counts.

At last you're getting out into the market and leveraging your network. It's a busy time. You'll need to take active steps and implement strategies to help you stay on track, maintain your energy and remain focused.

Let's leap into the market.

6
SHAPE
WHAT IS YOUR NEW CAREER IDENTITY?

*'We swallow with one gulp the lie that flatters us, and drink drop
by drop the truth which is bitter to us.'*
Denis Diderot

At the 99U Conference of 2013, vulnerability expert Brené Brown remarked, 'It's so scary to show up. It feels dangerous to be seen, it's terrifying. But it is not as scary, dangerous or terrifying as getting to the end of our lives and thinking, what if I had shown up? What would have been different?'[26]

Throughout her talk she referenced Theodore Roosevelt's famous 1910 speech 'The Man in the Arena', which is a powerful call to embrace challenge and give it a go, rather than becoming one of those 'cold and timid souls who neither know victory nor defeat'. Brené reminded us that if you are going into the arena, you will get your arse kicked from time to time, but that is better than sitting back and doing nothing.

If you're going to make a leap in your career,
you have no choice but to enter the arena.

The first two phases of this book focused on thinking about and planning your career leap, which is a lot of fun and relatively safe, as you can do much of it from the comfort of your lounge room or office. It would be easy to stop right here and keep dreaming, without actually getting out there and implementing the change.

But that's not you, because you want to leap! So let's look at what you need to do next to get your career into shape. And it starts by looking at YOU.

Identity crisis

I entered the new world of owning and running a consulting practice after leaving a senior executive position in the corporate world. This move was far harder than I expected. I was incredibly naive, wrongly assuming that to get the business rolling all I needed to do was tell a few people I was now working for myself. Initially I had no idea what I was specialising in and the service I was offering, so I couldn't clearly explain what I did. I didn't know how to position myself. I felt like a fraud, or like a three-year-old playing dress-up in clothes that didn't quite fit.

My connections, colleagues and even friends saw me in a certain light, and when I sought to step out of that light and head somewhere else many of them didn't know how to react, what to say or how to help.

I realised I had to get comfortable with a new identity: I was no longer a corporate executive but a business owner running a consulting practice. This didn't mean I changed my values or who I was as a person, but I had to alter how I saw myself as it related to my career, and how others saw me too.

A career leap means you are moving away from being one thing to being something else. For example, if you want to become a visionary leader who builds awesome teams, and you are seen as the technical expert who makes stuff happen, then there is a mismatch. If landing your next role requires you to be positioned as a deep thinker but you are best known for your operational expertise, then again there's a mismatch.

Look in the mirror

If you want to reinvent and reshape your career, and the market has a different view of you from the one you have, then it will be difficult to leap. Understanding your identity isn't a simple exercise. It is something we work on our entire lives!

For the purpose of your career leap, focus on how you see yourself in relation to the work you do now. Do you define yourself by your professional occupation or title? Do you define yourself by the status attached to your current role or the wow factor when you say what you do? How do you respond when someone in a social setting asks you what you do?

Much of how we see ourselves is shaped by the role we fill at work. It forms a crucial part of our identity. So when you change roles and move in a different direction, it is understandable that your identity will shift too, and you may feel uncomfortable with this.

The more you understand yourself, the value you offer, and what motivates and drives your behaviour, the easier it is for you to articulate what you stand for. Your ability to do that is crucial when crafting your positioning in the market and making a leap.

Ponder the following five questions and take some notes, as this will help you in exercise 6.1 (see p. 92):

1. How do you describe the work you do?

2. How do you think people describe you and the work you do?

3. How much status do you attach to your current role?

4. Will your proposed career leap change how you feel about the work you do, positively or negatively?

5. Does this worry you in any way? Why?

How do others see you?

Management consultant Tom Peters once said, 'All of us need to understand the importance of branding. We are CEOs of our own companies: Me Inc. To be in business today, our most important job is to be head marketer for the brand called You.'[27]

Some people hate the idea of thinking of themselves as a brand. They see it as inauthentic or even a bit crass. If that's you, then just remember your 'brand' is merely what springs to mind when people think of you. It's like the external version of your career identity—encapsulating what you are known for and your reputation.

> Your external career identity is your brand, which is your reputation plus the thing you are known for.

At its most primal level, your reputation is about whether people trust you or not. Are you of good character—someone who is consistent and reliable, for example? This self-assessment is important because if people don't trust you they won't be willing to recommend you, go out on a limb for you or help your career.

Your reputation can enhance or destroy your ability to leap. It also stays with you for a long time. It gets on the plane with you and leaps with you to the next destination, whether you want it to or not!

As Richard Branson put it, 'There is no denying the risk that mud sticks, and a damaged reputation in business can follow you around for years. You can deliver on every promise, keep your word, deal fairly, show forbearance—and the world can still throw you curveballs that mess up your reputation. And long after you have learned your lesson and moved on, others will still be harping on about this or that misfortune, this or that error.'[28]

There are three ways we generally categorise someone's reputation:

1. **Fictitious**—'It's all about me.' Your values are inconsistent and your behaviours are incongruent. What you say and do are often quite different. Your understanding of self and what drives your behaviour is usually low. Your reputation is poor.

2. **Fluid**—'It's all about pleasing the right people.' Your values are malleable and can shift as you seek cooperation and agreement from those in positions of power. You are easily influenced and can go against your own values. Your reputation is mixed.

3. **Evolved—'It's all about us.'** Your values are clear and transparent. You know what you stand for and are willing to back yourself in the face of criticism. You are also willing to listen to others, which means you can both hold ground and give ground. Your understanding of self is confident and purposeful. You have a strong reputation.

Obviously, your goal is to build an evolved reputation, but you may have some work to do to get there!

As well as your reputation, you will be known for something in your current market, typically the value or service you deliver. There will also be things you are not known for, which are usually at the opposite end of the spectrum. For example, in my corporate days I was known for getting things done and fixing problems, rather than as a strategist.

Are you best known as a strategic thinker or a details person, a leader or a team player, a thinker or a doer, an ideas person or an implementer, a technical expert or a creative thinker, someone who is people focused or who is task focused? What else would you add to that list as it relates to what you are known for?

Get real

The best way to find out how others see you is to seek honest feedback—warts and all!

Start by making a list of 10 to 15 people who know you in different areas of your life, including work colleagues, friends, family and contacts from community, voluntary or sporting associations. Aim for a broad mix of people who know you well and those who can offer insights into the initial impressions you make.

Ask each person for five words that spring to mind when they think of you. Then ask them to answer the following question: 'In one sentence, how would you describe me and the work I do?' Encourage them to be brutally honest and not to overthink the exercise. You may feel uncomfortable, surprised or even delighted by the responses. Regardless of how you feel, you will now have essential insights into what the market is saying about you.

In exercise 6.1 (overleaf), you will identify the points of commonality or misalignment between how you see yourself and how the market sees you.

To do this, look at the comments you wrote about yourself in the section on your identity ('Look in the mirror'), and compare them with the responses you've just received. Identify (1) any commonality or *alignment* in perspectives, and (2) any differences or *misalignment* in perspectives.

An alignment in perspectives won't necessarily help your career leap. For example, you may see yourself as a technical expert, and find others do too, yet your desired career leap destination requires that you be less expert and more focused on hands-on operations.

The same, of course, is true of any misalignment. In some cases, you may wish to work towards greater alignment, which means over time shifting how people see you. However, there may be areas where the market is ahead of you, and what needs to change is your *own* perspective on you.

You need to look at each element and work out whether the current positioning helps or hinders your career leap.

Exercise 6.1: Assess your current career identity

Fill in this table, noting where there is alignment and misalignment between how you see yourself and how others see you. Then consider whether that helps or hinders your career leap.

Career identity — areas of alignment	In what way does this help or hinder your career leap?

Career identity — areas of misalignment	In what way does this help or hinder your career leap?

A Cinderella fit

Now you have a greater awareness of how you see yourself and how others see you, you can figure out what you may need to shift or reshape to help you with your leap. This is about consciously crafting a position in the market that best supports your career leap.

If, for example, you are a corporate leader who builds great teams and you want to leap into a career running a café, then you will need to leave behind your corporate persona and get comfortable with the shift in status that will result. What you will want to take with you is your brand as a good leader, someone others want to work with and for. This will help you build an awesome team around you to make the café successful.

Getting your market positioning right is like shoe shopping. Not all the shoes you try on feel good, but if you keep trying you'll find the right fit and style. Always remember, however, that there is usually a bit of discomfort as you wear the shoes in.

Most importantly, you need to select the shoe that works for you—that represents your style. Don't let the market or what's in fashion dictate the style, colour or size you select. If you do, you'll end up becoming someone you don't want to be. You'll lose your identity and sense of self.

Authenticity is crucial. Research from Kellogg University shows that failing to be your authentic self causes psychological distress, which can have ongoing emotional and physical ramifications.[29] So heed the advice of Oscar Wilde: 'Be yourself; everyone else is already taken.'

Let's reflect on what you've found out about your career identity, and what you may need to shape or shift. This isn't easy to do, and it doesn't need to be done in one go. In fact, it's likely you will need to come back to this as you progress through the next stages of the Career Reinvention Cycle.

ASK YOURSELF

- Which elements of my career identity may need to shift, and in what way, to help me leap?

- How do I feel about shifting and reshaping those elements?

- What actions will I need to take to do that?

- Does this worry me in any way? Why?

- What can I do to overcome those concerns?

- How will I know my new career identity has landed well in the market?

As you move through the leap cycle, you will have moments of identity crisis. That's normal. Something may jar or feel wrong to you. When that feeling hits—and it inevitably will—come back and think about your identity. Consider what is making you feel like that.

Do you need to wear the shoes in for a bit longer, or are you wearing the wrong shoes?

Be honest with yourself and work out if you need to tweak your approach or take additional steps to get comfortable with your new positioning.

Your identity will shift

Simon Madden

Simon Madden was considered one of the finest ruckmen in the AFL, winning virtually every honour that elite-level football has to offer, including induction into Essendon's Hall of Fame and the AFL Hall of Fame. He started playing league football at 16, when it was seen as offering at best a part-time career, so when he left school he became a teacher.

'I retired from football when I was 34 and I then had to make a decision about what I was going to do. I initially went back to teaching, eventually becoming a vice principal, but knew I wanted to do something else. A friend of mine offered me a job in IT sales. I took that and moved up the ranks to account director for what was initially a small company but became Commander, a company with $1.4 billion in turnover. I was then headhunted for a role at Getty Images,' he says.

Now he's a specialist in building high performance in teams and individuals.

'A friend suggested I consider speaking and business coaching. That was 10 years ago and, with a few other side interests along the way, I now focus on helping people understand what it takes to be successful and what they have to do to stay there. This builds on what I saw in my sporting days. If you get everything else right — team, culture and the like — the scoreboard looks after itself.'

At each leap, Simon faced different challenges.

'When I moved from schoolboy football to what was then the VFL (now the AFL) I went from being a boy to a man and the expectations were different. When I moved from being a student to a teacher I started to understand what's important and to understand what it's like to be a teacher.

'When I stopped playing football there was the question of "What's next?" And yet so much of my identity was connected with being a football player. It was a big question to ask, but I needed to look forward and not backward.

'When I went into IT sales I used to go home and say to my wife, "I don't have a headache. I have a brain ache!" I was taking in so much new information it felt like my brain couldn't compute any more. It raised the inevitable fears of "Am I up to it?" You just have to face in to them and get over it. It's about getting clarity on the reality you are now in, and clarity on your identity.

'You are in control of your own destiny. When you have a real understanding of your attitude and do the work, you will get the result. It's about attitude, action and behaviour.

'Bite off more than you can chew, and then chew like hell.'

Write your new narrative

So who are you? A key part of shaping your new career identity is being prepared to stand up for your new career choice, and being known for something. This involves writing your new story.

You need to have a story that explains who you are, why you do what you do, and what you want to be known for. Think of it as your personal mission statement, leadership manifesto or leadership philosophy. Whatever you want to call it, it's your unique value proposition. It articulates the principles that guide your behaviour and the decisions you make.

We all carry baggage with us from prior experiences and our life history. These labels can box you in, confine you and stop you from standing out and being the best version of YOU.

Writing your story is your chance to discard any labels that are unhelpful and to shape a narrative that helps you succeed in your new career.

Herminia Ibarra (whom we met in chapter 2) has researched what can hold people, particularly leaders, back as they progress through their career. She found that our sense of who we are is shaped by our experiences and by the meaning we put on those experiences in terms of the stories we tell ourselves. At certain points in our career those stories are no longer helpful and we need to find a new narrative.

We all have defining moments in our life that have helped to shape who we are. These become stories that we tell ourselves and others. The danger arises when these stories hold us back, confining us to an outdated or unhelpful view of who we need to be. As Ibarra writes, 'we allow our stories, and the images of ourselves that they paint, to guide us in new situations. But the stories can become outdated as we grow, so sometimes it's necessary to alter them dramatically or even to throw them out.'[30]

The people I know who have done this really well have taken time to craft their statement. This is not a 'one hit and you're done' type of exercise. It takes time, effort and reflection. You'll know when it is close to the mark as you'll get goosebumps when you read it.

If you want to see a really good one, then check out my friend Jim Emerick's leadership philosophy at https://www.choinque.com/leadership-philosophy/.

Jim and I first met via Twitter and I have been continually impressed by how he lives out his leadership philosophy. It's not just a set of words—it embodies how he approaches life. When you read his narrative you get a very clear picture of who he is and what he stands for. He outlines his strengths and commitments, and is humble enough to share where he needs help. I particularly love the line 'You should know I'm a hopeless optimist, and may need your help to let me know when something just won't work'.

Now it's your turn to write your new narrative, as outlined in exercise 6.2.

Exercise 6.2: Write your narrative

Set aside some time alone in a space that is conducive to reflection. As you write your story, think about the past, present and future.

Ask yourself:

- What are the core milestones in my life — both positive and negative?

- How have they shaped how I see the world?

- When I look back over my life to date, what am I most proud of, and what am I least proud of?

- What does that tell me?

- How have my views of the world been formed?

- Who has most influenced my life. Why and in what way?

- How do I react when things go well, or not so well?

- What are the stories I tell myself about who I am?

- Do these stories help or hinder my progress? In what way?

- What matters to me and where do I want to leave my mark and really make a difference?

- What's my vision for the future?

- What do I want to be known for?

What comes up for you? What key themes emerge when you look at your answers? Use those details to start building a narrative about who you are, who you want to be, why you do what you do and what impact you want to have on those around you.

(continued)

Exercise 6.2: Write your narrative (*cont'd*)

Once you've spent time crafting and refining your narrative, the next step is to share it with a couple of trusted colleagues and friends. Get feedback from them, and find out what they think and whether they believe it sounds like you. Ask them how they felt when they read it. This is particularly important. You want people to feel something when they read it. It needs to evoke emotion and create a connection.

These words are going to underpin how you take yourself to market, so ideally when someone reads your manifesto they will say, 'I want to meet that person.'

Your narrative doesn't have to please everyone. You will never do that, and why would you want to? Your purpose is to be yourself, so if someone reads your narrative and doesn't like what you stand for, that's okay. You wouldn't want to work with them anyway!

A work in progress

Remember, shaping your identity, like working on your career, is a whole of life practice. We are all works in progress—we change as our environment changes. Our approach shifts as we evolve and the circumstances around us demand something more or something different from us.

So crafting your narrative is an iterative process, which means it needs to be constantly shaped and refined as you progress in your career.

CAREER CHECKPOINT

In this chapter you have been looking at your identity — how you see yourself and how others see you.

Let's check in on your progress before we move ahead to expand on this work:

- Are you clear on your current career identity and how you see yourself?

- Are you aware of how other people see you?

- Have you identified the gaps between how you are seen and how you need to be seen to support your career leap?

- Have you identified the action steps to take to close the gap?

- Have you written a first draft of your new narrative?

- Have you shared that narrative with trusted friends or colleagues and sought their feedback?

7
INFLUENCE
HOW WILL YOU ENTER THE MARKET?

'How very little can be done under the spirit of fear.'
Florence Nightingale

When I first entered the workforce, I was given a piece of advice by a family friend that has always stuck with me: 'It's not about always being the best when it comes to getting hired. People want to work with people they like. Be likable. If they like you, they'll hire you.'

This is still true today. You'll see it play out in hiring and promotion, sales and other business decisions, and your network's willingness to support you. Everything is just so much easier to do when people like you. When they like you, they are willing to help you.

You can't leap careers without getting yourself out into the market — meeting new people, seeking advice, finding advocates and getting job interviews.

Look at TV host Jimmy Fallon. He's certainly good, but a lot of people say he's not the best TV presenter out there. He's got one big thing going for him, though — he's incredibly likable.

He speaks highly of his competitors. He's sincere, authentic and down to earth. He listens, really listens, to what his interviewees have to say (unlike other presenters who talk too much while engaged in the conversation).

If you look at Jimmy Fallon's career, you'll see how he has strategically built the right networks to help him with his success. In a relatively short time, he went from being a cast member on *Saturday Night Live* to hosting *Late Night* to hosting the world's longest running talk show, *The Tonight Show*. And he has built a big network of followers (over 50 million) on social media along the way.

He has leveraged both his online presence and a loyal face-to-face network to progress his career. You need to do the same.

Impressions first

In today's marketplace first impressions count, not just face to face but also online. In fact, it's now more than likely your first encounter will be online. Before someone meets you for the first time, they'll Google your name and see what pops up. That could mean your website and social media images, as well as any incriminating Facebook photos of you.

Social media can be your friend or your enemy.

Sarah Wilson, of IQuitSugar.com fame, is a great example of how to make your online presence work for you when you're looking to leap.

Before becoming a best-selling author and entrepreneur, she worked as a journalist for 20 years. She started writing in her regular newspaper column about her experience avoiding sugar. An ebook followed, which led to a publishing deal and further books. As she built her business, she established clear positioning in the market on what she stood for and then leveraged traditional media and social media to help make her leap successful.

While you may not need to build a business or a brand the size and scale of Sarah Wilson's, you can't lurk in the shadows or be invisible online. It's nearly impossible! Whether you like it or not, social media is here to stay. You need to make sure that what is online is a true reflection of you and an accurate portrayal of your professional identity, supporting the role you want to create and obtain rather than the role you currently have.

Link in

You already know what you stand for and where you want your career to go. You've spent time considering your career identity and how it needs to be positioned. You now need to take that positioning to market, online.

At a minimum, for a career leap, you need a LinkedIn profile that clearly explains your value proposition—why you do what you do, what you do and how you do it. To help you craft the right profile, use your narrative from chapter 6 and your strengths from chapter 3.

Many organisations these days no longer look for CVs—they go straight to LinkedIn. The same applies to recruiters and anyone looking for prospective employees or service providers.

LinkedIn is also essential for deepening connections and broadening your network. I think of it as an online business card holder. Every time you meet someone, you should connect with them on LinkedIn, just as in the past you'd have handed them a business card.

It's amazing how many people you will find you know through others, and how you can leverage introductions through them. Coming recommended or referred by someone trusted can make all the difference to whether you land a new client or are interviewed and hired for a role. The biggest competitive advantage you have on LinkedIn is the number of recommendations you have for you and your work. Recommendations essentially act as an online reference, and the best thing is all you have to do is ask for one!

It's one thing talking yourself up; it's far more useful when someone else backs your skills, capabilities and competencies. Think of it as third-party support for the quality of the work you do and, most importantly, the calibre of you as a person. Remember, people hire people they like and trust!

Today's world works by ratings and recommendations. Expert360, an Australian startup, has created a website where companies can find workers for short-term projects based on their skill level and professionalism. If you go to sites such as Upwork, Guru, Freelancer and Fiverr, you can list your skills as a freelancer to source work from around the world and in multiple service categories. Sitting alongside your service description is a score, and a company or person will typically decide whether to engage you for a service based on that score.

The professionals on these sites know that a poor rating can affect how much business they get. I hadn't realised how much until I gave a designer I used a four-star rating, rather than the usual five. The service had been okay, but it wasn't up to the usual standard and we had to go back and forth many times to get it right. Within half an hour of my providing the rating I had an email from the designer saying they'd rather forgo payment for the job than have a four-star rating and would I be comfortable changing it to a five. For her, losing her five-star rating would seriously impact her business.

Looking good

If you have ever used an online dating site, then you will understand the importance of using a current photograph. This is true of your LinkedIn profile too.

Sure, we all want to look our best, but using a photograph that's 10 years old doesn't make you appear authentic. You may even come across as untrustworthy, which could potentially damage your reputation and put a stop to your leap. It's worth spending money to get a decent, accurate image to upload. Don't scrimp on this.

Having a dodgy pic is one thing; lying about your accomplishments and not being honest about your skills is much more serious—indeed, it can be viewed as fraud. So just as your profile's photo needs to match who you are, the words you use need to match who you are and what you do.

Extend your reach

Depending on the industry you are currently in, and the one you are looking to leap to, you may also need a presence on other platforms, such as Instagram, Facebook, Pinterest, Twitter and YouTube (and many others). Look at the industry sector and determine what's mandatory and what's optional.

For example, if you're a photographer it's essential to be on Instagram. If you're an online marketer or interested in the digital space, then you will need to show you have an understanding of these tools—which means being active on them. If you don't know how to use them, hire an expert to help you set up your profile and invest in some training as part of your leap.

For each of those platforms, consider what you can do to build engagement and awareness about who you are and what you do. Your positioning in the market will be defined by the type of content you like, share or post. It is a great way to build your profile, to stand out and be known for something, but you need to make sure it's the *something* you want to be known for.

You may not need to be on social media every day, but you do need a consciously cultivated presence.

As well, make sure the tone and style of your social media profile matches the industry or career you want to leap to. For example, if you are aiming to move from a corporate role to a role in the arts, then the tone of your profile and the images you use will be different. Similarly, if you are moving from the entertainment sector to a corporate role, you may benefit from adjusting your profile and images to be more in line with a corporate culture.

When you believe

Taking yourself to market is daunting and there will be times when you feel nervous putting yourself out there. In his best-selling book *Tribes: We need you to lead us*, Seth Godin suggests you need to create change that you believe in.[31]

As you make your change—your leap—you need to believe that:

- you can learn the skills and competencies you need to make the change
- you can make the career leap happen
- doing this leap will be good for your career and your life.

Your belief is your conviction. I love that word. If you don't have conviction as you take yourself into the market, it won't happen. People will pick up on your lack of self-belief. They'll feel your discomfort and uncertainty.

When you lack conviction, why would someone else be persuaded you are right for the job?

One of the best feel-good movies of the 1980s was *Working Girl*, a film that revels in big hair, form-defying shoulder pads and an awesome soundtrack. It's the story of Tess McGill (played by Melanie Griffith), a struggling secretary with big ambitions and the smarts to back them up. She does all the right things: goes to night school, seeks to broaden her network and is constantly looking for the next big idea.

She faces many hurdles, though, not least of them when her new boss, Katharine Parker (Sigourney Weaver), steals her big idea. When Katharine is later laid up in hospital with a broken leg, Tess seizes her chance to take herself into the market and make her idea happen.

The one thing Tess has in spades is conviction. Conviction that she is doing the right thing and that she will make it in her career in spite of the hurdles. As she says, 'You can bend the rules plenty once you get to the top, but not while you're trying to get there. And if you're someone like me, you can't get there without bending the rules.'

As you get into the market, you need Tess's chutzpah, her conviction without arrogance. And you need to be able to convey this online as well as face to face.

Power your position

It's said we have somewhere between 7 and 15 seconds to make an impression when meeting someone face to face for the first time. This conclusion is based on what is known in psychology as *thin slicing*. Professor Frank Bernieri of Oregon State University has found we assess people relatively quickly, without a lot of data. It might be from a glance, a handshake, what they wear, their demeanour or how they smile. We very quickly determine if we like a person and whether we see them as with us or against us.

Amy Cuddy, master of the 'Power Pose', has found that this first impression is based on our trying to answer two questions:

- What are this person's intentions towards me?
- How strong and competent is this person?

In doing so, she says, we make a judgement, first on how warm and trustworthy the person is and, secondly, on whether or not we think they're capable of acting on their intentions. These two trait dimensions, she believes, constitute 80 to 90 per cent of an overall first impression, regardless of culture.[32]

How you turn up each day matters. Your presence, your posture, your interactions and, most importantly, how you feel during those interactions. Amy Cuddy's research found that posture not only shapes the way we feel, it also influences the way we think. We are more likely to assert ourselves, seize opportunities, take risks and persist when we feel good.

'The way you carry yourself is a source of personal power—the kind of power that is the key to presence,' she explains. 'It's the key that allows you to unlock yourself—your abilities, your creativity, your courage, and even your generosity. It doesn't give you skills or talents you don't have; it helps you share the ones you do have. It doesn't make you smarter or better informed; it makes you more resilient and open. It doesn't change who you are; it allows you to be who you are.'[33]

One study looked at whether engaging in power poses would impact the outcomes of a job interview. The researchers were seeking to discover whether this practice would improve a person's presence, in turn leading to more favourable evaluations of their performance. The results: the people who did the power poses performed significantly better and were more likely to be hired.[34]

That's why Wonder Woman puts her hands on her hips; it explains Usain Bolt's signature stance known as the Lightning Bolt, and even why many of us throw our arms in the air after a win.

> A power pose can make you feel confident,
> even if you're not, and be especially helpful before
> a stressful job interview.

Find your crash mat

Andrew O'Keefe

Andrew O'Keefe pops up on your TV screen every Saturday and Sunday as co-host of Channel Seven's weekend *Sunrise* program. But before he was a household name, he worked in law at Allens Arthur Robinson.

Andrew leapt from the safety of a reputable job in copyright and trademark litigation to sketch comedy, game shows and then breakfast telly.

'I had no practical experience of TV whatsoever,' he admits. 'We'd also just bought our first house, and had our first child, so I was nervous. But I trusted that I was curious, affable and smart enough to work out the new business on the fly, and that my skills would more or less translate. That kind of confidence is indispensable.

'I've never taken big strides without stepping over some kind of chasm,' he adds. 'You have to trust your own skills enough to know you can fail and still find work. Even if that means, as a last resort, going back to what you were doing in the first place.

'I also discovered that people hire you because they want you and like you, so they're prepared to help you learn the ropes a bit through your failures. If you can build a rapport with a mentor you trust, you will never feel out of your depth.

'With confidence and good people around you, you have at least two crash mats. Which makes a big risk feel like a safe risk.

'I worked my pomegranates off for several years to catch up on what I'd missed through a lack of formal training. There is just no substitute for putting in the hours.

'You have to make sure that everyone you love is ready for it, so they will support you through it like a team of horses,' Andrew explains. 'It's not easy on your family ... they will be anxious and excited, and for the first time they may doubt your ability to carry it off. They need to feel a part of it all to counteract those fears.'

Search, scrutinise or shift

Various reports indicate that between 60 and 80 per cent of available jobs are unadvertised or sourced through a contact. For example, Interview Success Formula, a US company that runs programs to help people find new jobs, examined information from a range of sources including the US Bureau of Labor Statistics, CNN, UnderCoverRecruiter.com, GlassDoor and *The Wall Street Journal*. Their research showed that about 80 per cent of the 3.6 million jobs available in the United States at the end of 2012 weren't advertised.[35]

So your network is not just about who you know; it's about how willing those people are to help you with your leap. For example, would they put you forward for roles (which is why those LinkedIn recommendations are so crucial)? The data shows that 40 per cent of all hires in the United States come from employee referrals.[36]

Investing energy in your network will pay dividends,
as long as it is planned effectively.

There are three parts to successful network building:

1. **Search.** Who is in your corner and who isn't who should be?

2. **Scrutinise.** How will you build relationships and do you need to adopt a more progressive approach?

3. **Shift.** What actions should you take to build and leverage your network to help you make a successful leap?

Let's look at each of these in more detail.

1. Search

First you will want to craft a small and strategic group of people who will help to guide, challenge and inspire you through your leap. This is your personal advisory board. Its composition will change over time, so you need to know who's on it now, who's not on it (but should be) and who you need to retire from it.

This board may comprise five to eight people, ideally from a range of backgrounds and perspectives, providing different types of advice. They will also take on different roles, such as a *mentor* (who has been there and can provide advice on what the next steps may look like); *sponsor* (who advocates for you and will be in your corner cheering you on); *career coach* (who will be a sounding board and provide moral support and encouragement when it gets tough); *adviser* (who will offer advice on core aspects of the leap and may include a financial adviser, technology specialist and marketing adviser, for example); and *industry contact* (who will provide contacts in the sector you intend to leap to).

> Be prepared to pay for advice too. The best advice isn't always free.

Take a moment to think about who in your network is best placed to fill each of these roles for you. It may help to talk this through with colleagues or friends. There may also be people who aren't in your network — yet — who could play a role.

Once you've drawn up a short list of names, approach the people on the list and ask them if they'd be willing to provide advice and counsel. Some will accept, some decline, but don't die wondering — it can't hurt to ask. Just be clear on why you are approaching them, what you expect from them, and what they should expect from you in return.

Beyond your advisory board, you will want a broad, deep and established network. It will include stakeholders across a broad range of backgrounds and disciplines, both within and outside the organisation or area in which you currently work. A deep network runs across hierarchical levels, and is based on a mutual trust and willingness to provide support.

Taker, faker or maker?

As you plan and make your leap you will be surprised who will help you and who won't. When I made my move from corporate to setting up my own business, it was the people I least expected to provide support who did, often going to amazing lengths to help me land well. Yet others I thought I had very deep connections with provided no support at all.

I learned through experience that there are three types of people you will come across when you are looking to build your network and leap—the takers, the fakers and the makers.

You see these roles play out in characters on TV shows all the time. Let's use the HBO cult show *Game of Thrones* as an example:

- **Taker.** They say and do *anything* to get what they want. Cersei Lannister, widow of King Robert Baratheon and Queen of the Seven Kingdoms, is a great example. Everything she does is to further her ambitions. She sees the world as with her or against her: 'Everyone who isn't us is an enemy.' If you get in her way, she will seek to take you down.

- **Faker.** Their words and actions don't match. Lord Petyr Baelish, also known as Littlefinger, is a master manipulator who uses all his considerable wiles to gather intelligence on his rivals, amass wealth and garner power. He is dishonest and treacherous. He's also smooth and charming, but while he may act as though he is helping you, he works only for his own interests. His formula is: 'Always keep your foes confused. If they don't know who you are or what you want, they can't know what you plan to do next.'

- **Maker.** They are progressive and take action and step up for the good of all. Jon Snow, Lord of Winterfell and the Prince of Dragonstone, is one of the heroes of the story. He has strong principles and, while steering his own course, is sensitive to the needs of others. He is balanced in giving and taking, and is forthright and transparent in words and action, saying, 'If I don't take my own word seriously what sort of Lord of Winterfell would I be?'

In your network, the takers won't be as murderous as Cersei Lannister, but they won't help your career. Sure, in the short term there may be some gain if you give them something they need. But that's it. Don't expect loyalty or genuine interest, or any help at all unless there is an immediate and clear benefit for them. These individuals are usually quite easy to spot: they tend to be focused on themselves, manipulative and unhelpful, and can drain you of energy and throw you off course fast.

Fakers are often harder to spot. They're the 'wolf in sheep's clothing'. When you first meet them, you may be attracted to their apparent interest in you and your career. Over time, though, they won't live up to their promises, and as soon as someone else comes along who they feel will be more useful to them, you'll be dropped.

Both fakers and takers can enjoy short-term wins, but this type of behaviour isn't sustainable. The world is too small. It's the makers who will be genuinely interested in understanding you and your needs and be committed to building collaborative relationships. They understand that sustainable relationships require give and take and seek mutually beneficial outcomes.

It is the makers who will provide the support and guidance you need to advance your career leap. Makers have influence and are often well connected. They know the right people and will help you meet them. They will advocate for you while challenging your thinking. This is important, because you need to seek out people with different opinions to ensure your network has character and diversity.

You need to leverage support from the makers, while ditching or restricting the time you spend with takers and fakers.

Spend time identifying who you don't know but need to know. These may be people in industries or roles that are connected to the area you want to leap to. Generate the list of people you want to connect with and meet by talking to people in your network, doing research, and investigating the influencers and connectors in that sector.

Once you have built your advisory board and identified your network, it becomes easier to know where you need to focus your energy.

2. Scrutinise yourself

A network works both ways. If you were to scrutinise how you build and treat relationships, would you classify yourself as a faker, taker or maker? What would your friends, colleagues and peers say?

When you build your network you need to be a maker too. The American author and salesperson Hilary Hinton Ziglar, affectionately known as Zig Ziglar, once said, 'You can have everything in life you want if you will just help enough other people get what they want.'[37]

This advice challenges the way the world often operates. We live in a celebrity-obsessed society that can focus to an unhealthy degree on selfish interest. It's easy to get caught up with what you need and what other people can do to help you. If you want to step up and leap to your next career destination you should think more about what you can do for others than what they can do for you.

Robert Cialdini, author of *Influence: The psychology of persuasion*, has found that we have an innate desire to help those who help us. We like to return favours. This means that if you do something nice for someone they'll usually feel obliged to do something for you.

Think about these questions:

- How can you help a colleague or connection build their network? Is there someone you could connect them with?

- Have you got new knowledge or an insight that could help someone else?

- Can you provide useful advice to a colleague or friend about their career?

- Is there a relationship at work that is important to you and that you should invest more time in?

Janine Garner counsels in her book *It's Who You Know*, 'Be an example to others in your network and model the behaviour you seek in return...'[38] It comes down to the golden rule: 'Do unto others as you would have them do unto you.' If you want a great support base to help you make the leap, first you have to be prepared to help others. Always look for ways to help others. That's a prerequisite for building a network that works for you, not against you.

3. Shift your network

So what actions do you need to take to shift your network so it's best positioned to advance your career leap?

Make it easy for people to get to know you, do business with you, work with you, support you and follow you—whatever is necessary to help you make your career leap.

You can pick up some great ideas on how best to do that and to reach out to key people in your network from a very unlikely source—the Behavioural Insights team in the United Kingdom. Affectionately known as the 'nudge unit', they were the world's first government institution dedicated to using behavioural science to help make public policy decisions and redesign public services.

Their work encourages people to change their behaviour, nudging them to do something different. They see four key attributes as necessary for this behaviour change, and you can usefully apply the same four attributes to your career.

1. Make it easy.

You need to be easy to find and connect with. If you have no social media presence, it is hard for people to find you. If you are slow in responding to emails and phone calls, people will stop trying to connect with you and won't bother engaging with you. If the message of who you are, what you do and the value you offer isn't clear, people won't know how to work with you or support you.

2. Make it attractive.

I am not talking physical looks, although personal grooming does matter. I'm referring to how you stand out in the market. Be personable and memorable. When you reach out to people, tell them about your desire to make a career leap and that you'd love their advice. Most people like talking about themselves, so you will find many who are willing to share their thoughts and experiences.

At the end of each meeting, ask them if there is another person they think you should talk to. If you don't know the person they recommend, ask them if they'd be willing to make the introduction. This introduction needs to be personalised, professional and purposeful. Be grateful for the time the person is prepared to provide you, be clear on why you want to meet with them, and tailor the request so it shows you understand the person and what they do. Always follow up each meeting with a personal thank you note.

3. Make it social.

Leverage the power of social media, networks and relationships to establish yourself in your new market. Part of this is what Robert Cialdini calls 'social proof'. If a person can see someone else they trust or admire endorsing or supporting you, it is often easier for them to do the same.

4. Make it timely.

Be conscious of the best time to reach out and engage with people. Understand their habits and preferences and prompt people for support at appropriate times.

> To stand out from the crowd you must build relationships that sustain you through this leap as well as your next.

Strategise and leverage

Janine Garner

Janine Garner, an internationally acclaimed entrepreneur, keynote speaker and author, is the founder and CEO of the LBDGroup, a networking community that connects like-minded women to help them achieve extraordinary growth.

She's leapt across countries and continents and up the corporate ladder, but her leaps have always been well planned and strategically considered.

'Take a moment to make sure you are leaping for the right reasons,' she advises. 'Sometimes a person may be running away from something. I often tell people if you are thinking of leaping, just sit on it and determine if the grass really is greener there. Is it that your purpose and passion for the role has changed, or is it that you want to keep growing and evolving?'

You need to get your why clearly defined, and not rush the decision.

'Leaving a salaried position to become a self-funded business isn't easy. People look from the outside and have a perception of success. They fail to see the effort required, the compromise that's needed and the determination that's essential to building something from scratch.

'It requires big-picture thinking, strategic thinking and detailed planning. Don't just jump. Think it through.

'This includes knowing how much money you need. Build it up before you jump,' she says.

'Your network is crucial. It can be quite lonely when you are looking to leap. The most critical part is to get the right people around you at the right time. When you have the right people, they can help push you forward so you make the right decisions to take the right steps to reach your ultimate destination.'

CAREER CHECKPOINT

Leaping is a collaborative effort. You have to get out there, build your profile, get yourself known, and cultivate and nurture your network.

So what have you done to take yourself to market?

- Have you reviewed and updated your social media presence?

- Do your online presence and actual presence match?

- Have you practised your power pose?

- Have you established or started to build your advisory board?

- Do you know who you need to include or ditch from your network — the makers, takers and fakers?

- Have you looked at how you currently build relationships and what needs to change?

- Do you know how to build and activate a network that works for you?

8

FOCUS
HOW CAN YOU
MAKE EACH DAY
MATTER?

'If you take care of the minutes, the years will take care of themselves.'
Tibetan saying

There's a scene in the 1999 sci-fi movie *The Matrix* where the hero of the film, Neo (Keanu Reeves), must test the extent of his untried powers. He has doubts about his role in the simulated reality called the Matrix.

Morpheus (Laurence Fishburne), his mentor, believes in the Oracle's prophecy that Neo is the One, the person who will save humankind from subjugation by the sentient machines that created the Matrix. He encourages Neo to leap from one high-rise building to another to help awaken his understanding of his potential capabilities.

'You have to let it all go, Neo. Fear. Doubt. Disbelief. Free your mind,' says Morpheus, before he jumps and soars effortlessly between the two buildings.

Neo walks to the edge of the building, looks down towards the ground far below and mumbles, 'Okey-dokey. Free my mind.' He walks back to the other side of the building to give himself a runway. As he prepares himself he mutters again and again, 'Free my mind. No problem. Right.' He slaps his hands together, braces himself, runs, leaps … and plummets to the ground, face first.

Those watching the training jump are disappointed, most expecting a different outcome. Someone then points out, 'Everybody falls the first time.'

By the end of the movie, Neo is fully in touch with his capabilities. He can leap tall buildings, stop flying bullets in midair and alter the computer code that underpins the Matrix. He has mastered his powers.

Making a leap isn't easy, and you won't land it in one go.

You don't wake up one day and decide, 'I am going to change careers', and the next day make your landing. It may take three months, six months, a year or even longer. Once you have started your leap, it may feel like you're in mid flight for some time, or it may take further time to work out if you have landed well and are at the right destination.

There will be good days, even great days. And then there will be the days when you wish you hadn't got out of bed. With focus, practice and determination you will master the art of the career leap—your launch and landing. Every day counts towards your progress.

The tyrannies of progress

I was working with a senior leader who was looking to move up in her career and at the same time wanted to shift industries. There was a lot going on in her world—children, building a new house, the pressures of an already big role. A number of people around her suggested the timing wasn't right because she already had too much on her plate. She ignored their opinions and kept going forward.

One of her internal superpowers was her ability to tame the tyrannies of progress. She managed her inner dialogue, was incredibly efficient with her time and knew how to balance her energy levels so she could sustain herself through the shift.

You too can tame the three tyrannies of progress: *dialogue* (how to tame the little voice inside your head), *time* (how to make the most of your precious time) and *energy* (how you conserve it and sustain yourself through your shift).

If all three aren't used wisely you won't make your leap. If you start to doubt yourself when things go wrong and your inner dialogue is self-defeating, you'll never take off or you'll crash mid flight. If you waste time and procrastinate, you'll take too long to make progress and give up somewhere along the way. If you don't use your energy wisely, you'll burn out and end up nowhere but in bed recovering from exhaustion.

1. Dialogue

When making a career leap, you have to use your mindset to push through. It will never happen if you wait for all the i's to be dotted and t's crossed.

You'll never truly feel ready … you just have to do it!

Your inner dialogue has key character traits. It may be friendly and helpful or, at the opposite end, hostile and negative. It may repeat the same comments again and again, or it may shift its commentary based on the circumstances. It may be a voice of reason that helps you think things through, or it may focus on fear and hold you back.

It's your dialogue, so you get to set the tune and frequency. If you don't like the dialogue that's currently playing, turn down the volume or change channels. You'll never just switch off your internal dialogue. There will always be a channel that's on; the issue will be whether or not it's playing music you want to dance to.

You'll find times when you want to throw in the towel and give up, but giving up is easy. Keeping going is harder, and it's by persisting that your efforts will pay off.

Take Sam Stosur, for example. She is one of Australia's most successful female tennis players, yet there is often talk that she has never quite lived up to expectations in her career. She has never quite landed the expected wins on home soil, and she has never got beyond the fourth round in the Australian Open. But she beat Serena Williams in 2011 to win the US Open and reached the French Open final in 2010. She is also a former world No. 1 in doubles, a ranking she held for 61 weeks, and a former world No. 4 in singles.

Despite what the media report about her, Sam Stosur keeps going. She has also never just thrown in the towel or admitted to being 'bored', as Bernard Tomic did after his first-round Wimbledon defeat in 2017.

Exceptional athletes know how to push through. They understand the mental fortitude required for peak performance, recognising that half the battle is their mindset. It's the same with your career leap.

Affirm and learn

One way to help ensure your mindset serves you is through self-affirmations. Before you roll your eyes, this is more than just standing in front of the mirror every day and saying, 'I'm awesome'. It's about how you look at the world and reframe it when something doesn't work out.

Self-affirmation is a psychological theory originally proposed by Claude Steele. It's based on the belief that people are motivated to maintain their self-integrity—that is, a positive view of themselves. That makes perfect sense. You want to think and feel you are a good person. When your view of your 'self' is threatened you'll do things—adapt or change your behaviour—so your positive self-image is restored and you go back to feeling good about yourself. These threats to your self-image may be either real or perceived failures to meet a desired social or cultural standard or expectation.

In the context of a career leap these might be, for example, a knockback for a job you applied for, or someone you admire questioning or challenging your shift in careers.

There are different ways of approaching these threats. One way is to accept the situation and find ways to change your behaviour to adapt to the threat. Another way is to change how you interpret the situation so it becomes less threatening to your self-image. In the case of a job knockback, for example, this could mean you put the failure down to the interviewer, rather than considering what you might need to do differently next time.

This approach is 'defensive' in nature, as you seek to alter the meaning you place on the event in a way that protects you from thinking that your beliefs or actions were misguided.[39] When this happens you don't learn from the experience; rather, you seek to blame others or explain away what happened. This is not helpful for your career leap.

A more useful response when something goes wrong is to do one or more of these three things: reflect on what's really important to you, engage in activities that reinforce the values most important to you and focus on your strengths (which you identified in chapter 3).

The key is that these actions aren't directly related to the threat. When you do this, you'll realise your self-worth isn't based on your evaluation of what's just happened.[40] You won't view yourself as a 'failure'; rather, you'll simply recognise that this time you weren't successful. This helps to reduce the impact of the event while enhancing your internal resources, making it easier to cope with what has happened. You'll also broaden your perspective on what has happened, making you less likely to brood on the issue.[41]

Benjamin Franklin was already a master of this approach when he said, 'I haven't failed. I've had 10,000 ideas that didn't work.'

2. Time

Time is like money: once it's spent you can't get it back. You can't spend 'future' time because you can't spend what you don't have. You can only spend time you currently have. By this line of reasoning it is the present you should be most concerned with, because it is only present time you can be certain you have. This isn't so with your career leap.

Instead, think of time as like a triangle with three elements — past, present and future. To make a great career leap you need to use all three wisely. Reflecting on the past helps with learning. Thinking about your future helps with goal-setting and ensuring you are staying current and focused on what is changing around you. Being present and using your time wisely helps advance you towards your life and career goals.

It's about balance. You need to look behind you, but not for so long that you get lost in the past. Reflecting on past experiences and examining what to do differently next time is critical for career change. However, becoming fixated on something that has passed and that you cannot change is unhealthy and a waste of your precious time.

If you concentrate only on the present and live for the moment, you'll spend no time looking ahead and you'll ultimately get left behind. It's important to continually scan the horizon so you can see what is changing and what you need to do to stay ahead of the game. At the same time, if you only focus on the future you'll miss what is around you. You'll miss being present and the benefit of making each day matter.

Often the hardest time to tame is the present. What you do or don't do each day matters. You are about to embark on a career leap and it won't happen if you sit around in your PJs, eating chocolate or drinking red wine all day. You need focus—and lots of it.

Focus is easier when you are clear on your ultimate goal and what you need to achieve each day to make that goal happen.

This helps you avoid distractions and activities that divert your attention away from your purpose. You want to suck the marrow out of every single day and use your time wisely. In his book *How to Lead a Quest*, Jason Fox writes about the siren call of self-sabotage and identifies seven warning signs: procrastination, perfectionism, being busy, disorganisation, over-commitment, physiological self-sabotage and choosing difficult circumstances.[42] While he was writing in a different context, his list is beautifully relevant to this situation and your desire to leap.

It's easy to procrastinate. We loll around waiting in the vain hope that motivation will strike. We tell ourselves, 'I just need to do this other [less important] thing, and then I'll get cracking.'

We have this strange notion about motivation, convincing ourselves it comes through moments of inspiration, the a-ha moment or the lightning bolt. It doesn't! Motivation comes from starting. Just get up and go, whether you feel like it or not. You will have days when it will be hard to keep going, so keep your eye on the prize and just keep moving forward.

If you are a perfectionist (and yep, I place myself firmly in this category), there will never be a perfect time to leap. You have to ditch the notion of perfectionism. This doesn't mean you do a half-hearted job and turn up unprepared. It does mean you will go to market before you feel ready. And it does mean you will leap before you feel truly ready.

You won't have all the knowledge or skills you need. You won't have a perfect LinkedIn profile, social media platform or service offering. These are always works in progress.

It's about just having enough — your minimum viable level of readiness — and then getting going.

Make each day count

Being busy on things that don't matter and being disorganised won't help your leap either. Making each day matter is about planning ahead.

Don't just write a list of what you have to do each day. Instead, work out how many hours you will 'work' during the day, then for each 30-minute block write down what you want to do in that time—whether it's connecting with a certain number of people or setting up a meeting to chat to someone in your new industry.

Once you've completed a task, cross it off your list. This simple approach helps you maintain a sense of progress so the brain's natural reward chemical, dopamine, kicks in.

When you are leaping, your time is precious. You are devoting time to another area of your life, so you have no choice but to be deliberate about what you take on and to prioritise ruthlessly.

Prioritising means not over-committing and learning to say no. You simply can't accept every invitation that comes your way. Be clear on which social activities you need to scale back. Doing this will help you create space for thinking and doing, as well as time to keep yourself physically and mentally alert. Creating difficult circumstances, to use Jason Fox's words, isn't going to serve you.

ASK YOURSELF

- Am I conscious of how I'm using my time?

- Is it purpose driven and focused, or is it completely random and misdirected?

- Will the activities I do today get me one step closer to my career leap destination?

- How much time am I wasting on activities that don't add any value?

- What can I stop doing to create space to devote to my leap?

- How do I better prioritise my day so I do what matters most first?

Henry David Thoreau wrote, 'It's not enough to be busy. So are the ants. The question is, what are we busy about?'

3. Energy

Your career leap takes work, and a lot of thinking. You need to use your brain's capacity wisely.

I liken the thinking part of the brain (the pre-frontal cortex) to a battery. As you sleep it recharges, but as soon as you get up in the morning and start doing work that requires you to think, analyse and process information, that battery starts to drain. So by the end of the day the battery is pretty low.

You use your brain wisely by focusing on the most energy-intensive tasks—important phone calls or industry research, for instance—in the morning, when you are most alert. You also don't waste your brain's energy on things that don't matter, such as checking Facebook or getting a haircut, unless it's needed for that important job interview!

It has been suggested that during his time in the White House, Barack Obama owned only two types of suits. The logic? Why waste mental energy on choosing what to wear each day? Even if that story is fiction it's a great example of using your brain wisely!

A key tip is to not follow the fallacy of multitasking. Research shows the only thing that multitasking does is ensure you take longer to get your core task done. Turn off all electronic distractions so you are focused on one thing at a time. There are even apps to help wean you off frivolous activity that you can't resist. Apps such as Forest, Freedom, Anti-Social, Cold Turkey and TrackTime all seek to help you be more productive.

> ## Focused activities, being deliberate with your time and not multitasking, will help you advance your career leap.

I take this approach to every workday, while also scheduling in time for exercise and 'down time', both of which are critical. When you are busy it can be hard to prioritise *you*, but your body needs time to rejuvenate to ensure it operates at peak performance.

If this sounds structured, it is! What I can tell you is it can shave hours off your workday. You'll be way more productive, and less likely to waste time and energy on irrelevant activities.

PATIENCE IS A VIRTUE

Marc Alexander

Marc Alexander has made a number of career leaps, through transport, logistics, offshore commercial fishing, winemaking and retail sales roles. His biggest and most recent leap was moving from being a music teacher and professional performer to working in financial services.

'This current transition has taken approximately 30 months of constant, steady effort, so I've had to refocus myself from a sprint (my natural tendency) to a marathon,' he says. 'That was hard.'

Staying the course when the leap takes a long time is challenging. There were a number of key things that helped Marc.

'Be patient,' he advises. 'Believe in yourself and your direction. Seek professional career advice. Take counsel from those already in your target area. Build relationships with connected and progressive leaders in your new industry, and learn your target industry's language — read broadly and deeply.

'I look back at many of the roles I applied for and didn't get, and feel so grateful that those pathways didn't continue. I'm so lucky to be where I am now,' he adds. 'Hindsight is a fabulous thing!'

Make it work

Perhaps you have already decided to leave your job to pursue your leap wholeheartedly. Great! That means your leap *is* your new job and you need to treat it as such.

You have a destination and a plan. You know where you are going and have mapped out the key steps to get you there. You've packed your bags, but you are not yet ready to head to the airport to catch your flight. There are still more things you need to do before you leap, including meeting key people, researching, preparing for and going to job interviews, or perhaps building the infrastructure required to get your business off the ground.

> If you decide to stay in your current job until you are a bit more prepared, then you need to make work work for you.

You must continue to work effectively and deliver value to your employer. You can't let your current job suffer, along with your reputation, just because you've decided you want to do something else. It won't help you in the long run.

The best thing to do is look for opportunities to create connection points, or areas of overlap, between your current work and where you want to leap. These connection points may be knowledge or skills you can acquire or people you can meet. You might get an opportunity to go on a course and build more skills that could help you when you transfer.

Become the master of your job role. Be strategic about any extra work you take on or projects you get involved in. Pick the ones that are most likely to help you. This is your discretionary effort, so use it wisely.

For example, if you want to move into project management and you currently work in communications, see if there is a small communications project you can get involved with. If you want to move out of corporate and into the consulting world, find ways to spend time with people at work who have been consultants and see what you can learn from them.

You may have to juggle your current work along with job interviews, meeting people, researching, developing and planning your exit—another reason why it's important you manage your dialogue, time and energy effectively!

Negotiate your leap

Throughout the Career Reinvention Cycle, you'll need to develop your negotiation skills, whether in relation to a new contract or working arrangement, a business agreement, or how and when you exit your current role. A failure to negotiate well can have a huge impact on how you land your leap.

The three core elements here are *readiness* (being prepared for the negotiation, especially if it's about the dollars), *relationships* (understanding the relationships involved and seeking mutually beneficial outcomes over the long term) and *resolve* (having the tenacity to see it through to a satisfactory conclusion).

Get ready

Successful negotiators know they can't just 'wing it' and hope for a good outcome. You are far more likely to achieve your goals if you're ready for the conversation.

This, again, requires you to prepare your mindset. You'll be pushed and pulled in many directions as you leap. If you go into a discussion prepared (but not locked in) for 'this' to happen, you will be better positioned to respond to 'that' and whatever else comes your way.

If you can maintain a calm demeanour and manage your feelings, your mind will be much better equipped to handle the discussion. If, on the other hand, your pre-frontal cortex (the thinking part of the brain) is overpowered by 'fight or flight' triggers (that is, the emotional centre of the brain) or is simply tired, you'll be less able to make reasoned and well-considered decisions. Your wise one will have abandoned you!

When you are entering a new career, a negotiation can feel harder than it might have felt in the past. This is because you're dealing with a new range of uncertainties. You may be uncertain about how much money to ask for, as you don't know what the market pays. You may be worried that if you negotiate too hard, they'll withdraw the offer and you'll lose what may feel like your one chance to make the leap.

If it's taking a long time to make the leap, you may feel pressured just to take what you can get so at least you've landed somewhere.

Your fears can be minimised when you know your worth and value, and what you bring to the new role.

This starts with talking to people in the market and finding out what's standard practice and the going rates. There will be a low entry point and a high entry point. If you ask for too little, people will worry that you aren't any good at what you do. If you go too high, you may price yourself out of the running.

Find the sweet spot, which will usually be more than you feel comfortable asking for. If you are totally comfortable with the figure, it's likely you are going in too low. Sure, you may not have worked in this field before, but throughout your career you have demonstrated that you learn quickly, add value, make an enormous contribution and deliver great outcomes.

Think of yourself as a luxury product. Ensure your packaging matches your price. This isn't about expensive clothes and designer-wear; it's about being well groomed and professional and having all the behavioural attributes of the role you aspire to.

Think long-term relationships

Negotiating effectively is much easier if you have a good relationship with the person or persons involved. This isn't always feasible when you are leaping between careers. What you can do, though, is find out as much as possible about the people you will be negotiating with. These insights will help you understand what they are likely to reject or support. Talk to people who know them or, even better, people who have negotiated with them before. Seek to understand their operating style and what they care about. Most importantly, know the currency that matters to them.

Equipped with these insights, you can present your pitch on the value you offer in terms of how it will help them succeed and satisfy their needs. You are far more likely to be successful if you can show that what you are asking for will benefit the other person or the organisation, not just you. You want them to walk away from the process feeling as though they have done well. This means you need to be reasonable and not ask for something they can't give you.

Also, be wary of accepting the first offer that is put on the table. It is a strange quirk of human nature that if we accept the first offer made, the other person is likely to feel unsatisfied. They infer that because you accepted too readily they should have gone in harder or that they've been too generous.

Learning to negotiate effectively will set you up for when you're dealing with potential employers, clients, customers and, of course, your current boss. It's likely you'll have to negotiate your exit from your current organisation (more on that shortly).

See it through with resolve

You may *feel* that because you are starting out in a new industry or role you have fewer chips to bargain with, but you actually have more than you think.

It's easy to see why the person with positional authority or status—it may be the person doing the hiring, your first potential client or a critical supplier—tends to believe they have more power in the relationship. This feeling of power gives them strength, so they negotiate harder.

Feeling more powerful can impact how you negotiate too. The key word here is 'feeling'.

When we feel more powerful, we are more powerful, and we get better outcomes when we negotiate.

Dutch researchers lain Hong and Per van der Wijst, of Tilburg University, found this to be particularly true for women. Participants in a study were asked to recall times when they had power, while a different group were asked to write about how they spent their evenings.

The participants then went into a series of negotiations together. Results showed that women who were primed to feel powerful made much more aggressive first offers and negotiated better outcomes for themselves than women who did not. Interestingly, men reached similar outcomes whether or not they were primed to feel powerful.

The good news is we can all *feel* more powerful. Here are some practical shortcuts:

- Practise Amy Cuddy's power poses, discussed in chapter 7.

- Sit up straight, because your posture impacts your behaviour and how confident you feel.

- Tap into your inner sense of power, which comes from knowing who you are and liking yourself.

- Make sure you get enough sleep and exercise, and eat well, because feeling physically fit and mentally alert enables you to manage yourself better and feel equipped to get the best out of a negotiation.

When you negotiate, be deliberate about what you want. It's often simply a case of 'Don't ask, don't get'. You'll never get something if you aren't first willing to ask for it. State your wants objectively by using statistics, data or objective measures that are hard for the other party to ignore.

Try to remain emotionally detached from the outcome. This isn't easy, particularly if the issue really matters to you. However, the more attached you are to a predetermined outcome, the harder it will be to negotiate.

Negotiation involves give and take—it's not all about you. To be successful you will need to be prepared to give things up or trade something to get something else that matters more to you. For example, if you are negotiating working conditions you may be willing to trade money for flexibility, or money for extra holidays.

It's easier to do this when you are clear about your boundaries and priorities. These are your non-negotiables, including the point at which you will walk away from the discussion.

> While you need resolve to negotiate effectively,
> you also need to know when to walk away.

Manage your exit

As you negotiate your landing in your new destination, you also need to negotiate elements of your exit from your current working arrangement, if you have one. You may have to negotiate the date you will cease employment, for example, in order to leave earlier or later than stipulated in your contract.

Be prepared to be let go on the spot. Some organisations bent on protecting their intellectual property may walk you out the door immediately, especially if you are moving to a competitor. This is done less frequently these days, but it's best to be prepared.

Have everything sorted out beforehand so if they do decide to walk you out, all you need to do is go back to your desk and collect your personal items. And don't feel like it's a walk of shame. Respect their decision (even if it seems silly), so you can preserve relationships as best you can. Don't burn your bridges. You want to exit with dignity and grace, not with your middle finger in the air.

Three cardinal career moves to avoid are *dummy spits*, *productivity sags* and the *dump-and-run*. It's likely you've seen most of these play out before. Someone who doesn't handle the exit well, and they tell their boss, and everyone who will listen, how glad they are to be going and how they can't stand working there. The 10 minutes of pleasure you might get from telling it like it is, or telling someone exactly what you think of them, isn't worth it. It will come back to haunt you.

While you may not have enjoyed the role or liked your boss, it doesn't mean you won't need certain relationships later down the road. It's a small and very connected world.

Many years ago, in an organisation I worked for, a colleague sent a long email to an internal distribution list explaining why he was leaving, what he disliked about the organisation and why it was doomed to fail. While some of his points may have been valid, it left his colleagues feeling hurt and, in some respects, angry. There is a much better way to communicate your exit — without destroying your reputation, and hurting your friends and colleagues along the way.

Sure, once you've decided to go, it can be hard to maintain your enthusiasm and productivity as you prepare to exit the front door. It's natural that your brain starts to switch focus from your current to your new role. Your attention is squarely on the future and how exciting that looks. In the meantime, though, you are frustratingly stuck in the past, doing what you have done for so long and very much want to leave behind you.

If you stop working productively it will impact how your colleagues see you. They will remember that you just 'faffed around' and wasted time after you resigned. They also won't appreciate the impact it has on them, as it's likely they'll be left to pick up the work you don't do or do well.

Doing the dump-and-run won't help your colleagues, and it won't paint you in a favourable light either. You store up all the really challenging or problematic work then, in your handover meeting, you gleefully handball it all to the person who is managing the role going forward or until a replacement is found. Naturally that person feels annoyed that you have passed them a load of crap that you should have at least tried to fix or resolve before you left.

It may not be possible to tie everything up with a neat bow, but wherever you can, be sure to resolve issues and bring work to the nearest possible point of completion.

Never forget, managing your exit is as important as managing your entry into an organisation or new career.

CAREER CHECKPOINT

This wraps up phase 3. You've spent time getting yourself ready to leap, shaping your new identity, building your positioning in the market, and working every day on the activities you need to do to ensure your leap lands well.

In the next phase, you'll really start to take off. But before you do, let's recap:

- Are you working through the challenges you confront as you prepare your leap?

- Are you managing your time and energy effectively?

- Are you looking for opportunities to leverage your current work to aid your leap?

- Have you readied yourself for the key negotiations you will need to undertake as part of your leap?

- Have you started to think and enquire about salary or work arrangements for your next career destination and how you will negotiate what you want?

- Have you managed or planned your exit well?

PHASE 4
ACCELERATE
How will you leap quickly and successfully?

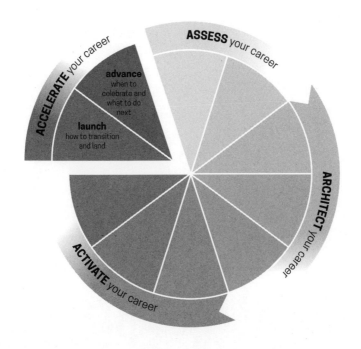

In this final phase, you'll leap to your new destination!

Each leap takes a different length of time to complete, and you may be 'in flight' for a while. You'll need to prepare yourself for turbulence, as well as a bumpy landing.

It's important to remember that the Career Reinvention Cycle is not just something you go through once and then forget. You will use it to leap multiple times. Even when you think you've 'made it' there is more work you can do to ensure you remain future fit.

9

LAUNCH
HOW WILL YOU TRANSITION AND LAND?

'The art of knowing is knowing what to ignore.'
Rumi

There's no denying that Sir Richard Branson, founder of Virgin, launches big, proud and loud. When he enters a new industry or promotes a new product, it's not done under the radar. It's a carousel of flashing lights and fanfare. He has driven a tank down Fifth Avenue in New York, shaved his beard and donned a bridal gown, and posed in a space suit, as Elvis and as a Zulu warrior. When he jumped off the roof of a Las Vegas casino hotel to promote Virgin America, he crashed into the side of the building twice, ripping his pants. Later he laughed it off, saying, 'I never thought I would take the saying "flying by the seat of my pants" quite so literally.'[43]

While your launch, your leap, shouldn't require a jump harness, a stunt double or even new pants, it does require guts, determination and confidence.

You are now committing to turning your back on your old role or career, and leaping into the wind, so to speak. What this looks like in practice will vary according to each individual's unique experience. Your take-off and someone else's will be slightly different, as will every leap you make in future.

You may have a new role lined up, but you haven't yet started. Or there may be a number of roles actively in play, none of which you have yet landed. Or you may have a business idea in development that isn't yet in the market. Perhaps you have reached the point where you are feeling ready to leave the security of what you know to focus your energy solely on your leap. Alternatively, you may have been working the dual track for some time and are now ready to hit the single runway.

> Whatever your destination, whichever runway you are taking, it's time to board your flight.

Pre-flight check

I find travel really exciting, though some people find it boring or, if they fear flying, highly stressful. It's natural at this stage to have pangs of doubt or uncertainty, wondering, 'Am I getting on the right plane?' or 'Am I really even ready for take-off?'

Exercise 9.1: Do your pre-flight inspection

If you're feeling unsure about whether you are ready, complete this pre-flight checklist to get you ready to board:

- Do I have a general destination?

- Am I clear on my market positioning?

- Do I have a network in place, or in development, to support my leap?

- Are my finances in place to support my leap?

- Am I prepared to accept the risks and make the tradeoffs associated with this leap?

- Is my learning program underway?

- Is my plan for my leap progressing well?

- Have I nailed enough key elements of my business plan to get things off the ground (if I'm flying solo)?

If you have answered 'no' to any of these questions, ask yourself:

- What isn't in place and what needs to be?

- Does that really stop me from boarding my flight, or can I catch up later?

Your destination may be clear, but the route you'll take and how you'll land may feel unresolved and risky. Many people take off still unsure of precisely where or how they will land. Even if you've already got a job lined up, and are raring to go, there is a chance that things won't go according to plan.

When I left corporate, having decided to start my own business, I knew what I liked doing and what I was good at, so I developed Change Meridian as a business that would help organisations, teams and individuals thrive in a complex, challenging world. I thought I would provide advice and guidance to help people better manage organisational change. After a few years I found myself not shifting countries, but moving just a few suburbs over. I've refined my value proposition and services. I still work in the context of change, but with a focus on helping organisations, teams and people get fit for the future of work. Now here I am writing a book on career leaps.

Don't fall into the perfectionist trap, believing you have to have absolutely everything mapped out and in place before you board.

Often when you travel, you find you have left something behind that you meant to bring with you, but it doesn't stop you from getting on the plane. You'll just restock when you get there.

There are, of course, essential items you'll need, such as your passport and wallet, or in this case an actionable plan and viable strategy to implement the key steps in your leap. But a lot of the details can be dealt with while you are in flight or when you land. You may have more interviews to do, people to meet or learning to complete. You may have to do more work on setting up your business or developing your product.

Once the flight attendant announces the cabin doors are closed and you begin to taxi towards the runway for take-off, you need to buckle up, sit back, enjoy the ride and get ready for the in-flight experience.

In midair

You may be making a quick trip and landing, like a promotion to the next department, or it may be an extended solo expedition with lots of stopovers on the way, which can feel like you're in flight for quite a while. How long your leap takes is actually irrelevant. What matters is that you have your navigation system switched on to ensure you are keeping on track. For this to work, you need to have loaded the right coordinates, and to monitor it regularly.

Consider: Do you have the right support to help you course correct as you progress? Are you checking for changes in market conditions that might affect you? Whose advice are you listening to? Not all the counsel you receive from your advisory board and people you meet will be helpful, so be discerning.

Stay tuned in to how the market is behaving and you'll hear or see ideas that you can tailor or leverage. You may meet other people who are on a similar journey to you, and perhaps you can learn from them. As you do this you may identify points where you need to adjust your course slightly to ensure favourable conditions, and an even better landing.

It's important to make adjustments when you need to as you progress. To maintain forward momentum, keep your plan from chapter 5 visible. Monitor your action steps and identify what you may need to devote more attention to. Be clear on which action steps are adding the most value in helping you to progress your leap.

If you focus solely on ticking all the boxes, you may miss an interesting opportunity that could add value to your leap.

Consider applying the 80–20 rule. Essentially, the Pareto principle, derived from the work of the Italian economist Vilfredo Pareto, shows that roughly 80 per cent of effects come from 20 per cent of causes. In the context of a career leap, identify the 20 per cent of your effort or time that is creating 80 per cent of the impact, then (if necessary) adjust the focus of your attention accordingly while you're in flight.

This will also help you see which activities are least productive, and therefore could (or should) be stopped or reduced. The key is not to waste your energy at this point in the cycle on things that don't matter.

Turbulence and what to do about it

Not every flight will be smooth. In fact, most are a bit bumpy! When you hit bad weather, it can be easy to start to lose confidence in yourself and wonder whether you will ever land safely. Stay strong and remind yourself why you decided to board the plane in the first place. Strap yourself in and focus on your destination. It helps to have in place something that makes it harder for you to turn back.

If you've ever worked on the implementation of a major IT system, you'll know that one strategy for dealing with resistance is to quickly shut down the old system once the new one has been launched. By doing this, people have no choice but to get over the discomfort of learning to use a new system. Forced to overcome their fear of the unknown, they adapt faster and keep moving forward.

When things get tough and you're searching for the exit, what do you need in place to make it harder for you to go back to your old work ways? If you've quit your job or you've been made redundant, it's likely you don't have the option of going backwards. The reality is your best way forward is to make your leap work for you.

For others, the solution may be going public. When you tell others about what you are doing it becomes harder to turn back—so tell everyone! Better still, get an accountability buddy to check-in with your progress each week. At those check-ins, talk about what you committed to do during the past week, and what you actually achieved. Then set new commitments for the following week. A buddy can help keep you on track by challenging you when you default on commitments and encouraging you to navigate through them.

Buckle up
Sandy Hutchison

When you leap, you leave some things behind. For Sandy Hutchison, CEO and founder of the startup Career Money Life, it was a successful corporate life as the Asia-Pacific human resource director of Marsh &

McLennan Companies, a New York–based global professional services firm of 60 000 people.

While this wasn't her first leap, it was her biggest.

'Going from being part of a large, prestigious company to being alone with an idea and not much else is daunting,' she admits. 'You need to draw on a great deal of inner resilience and self-belief, much more so than you would imagine. With the lack of regular contact with others and as the structure and routine that is your daily life in a corporate falls away, you need to create new routines and structures that are entirely self-imposed. It can be hard to be both employee and boss, with only you to hold yourself to account.'

'The most challenging stage of a career change is at the point of departure, when you are still connected to the past and what was, and not yet clear on what the future will be. This period can be stressful and emotionally draining,' she says, 'especially so if you are creating something new, like a startup.'

Sandy found she needed to create external structures to support her, including an advisory board.

'There is a tradeoff here for anyone setting up a business, and I think I should have got more help from others. You need to know your strengths and focus on those, getting other people to do the rest, otherwise you can spend a lot of time unproductively.'

Sandy learned a lot though the process, including the need to be simultaneously patient and persistent.

'When creating a new product, it takes time to build a client base. I have had to learn not to take rejection personally, and to meet the challenge of turning no into yes over time. This draws on a great deal of internal strength and self-belief, which can sometimes be hard to muster.

'Starting your own business is both exciting and terrifying at the same time, a bit like a roller-coaster ride—in fact, a lot like that, with many ups and downs. I love what I am doing and after three years of hard work, I am seeing the rewards.'

Embrace touchdown

Before attempting to land the plane, the pilot runs through a landing checklist to ensure nothing has been forgotten. There are lots of variables to consider:

the weather, crosswinds, visibility and turbulence. These factors, plus the pilot's experience, all combine to affect how well the plane hits the tarmac.

Interestingly, a good landing isn't always a smooth landing. Too soft a touchdown may indicate that the plane has not fully landed and can still be pushed back into the air. The landing is complete not when the wheels first hit the tarmac, but when the plane has slowed down and is taxiing towards the gate.

It's the same with your career landing: it doesn't stop until you're well and truly at the gate. You need to be prepared for this. You may think you're about to land (and start your new job), when the plane suddenly bounces up again because the conditions aren't quite right (your new job falls through).

I've been through this before, both on a plane and in my career, and it's not fun. You feel you are so close, then you're not! Just as you trust the skills of the pilot to land you safely, trust your own skills and capabilities to see you through to a safe landing—eventually. It just may mean you'll be in flight a little bit longer than you expected.

It may also mean you need to make a slight adjustment to your flight plan, like Mary Kay Ash, the founder of the billion-dollar empire Mary Kay Cosmetics.

At age 45, Ash was annoyed that she was constantly passed over for promotions in favour of male employees (some of whom she herself had trained). So she quit her sales role and set up her own company, though this hadn't been her original intention. Initially she set out to write a book about sales, but she spotted a business opportunity.

She then used her life savings to create a direct selling company focused on beauty creams. Since 1963 her company has grown to an incredibly successful business with millions of independent beauty consultants selling her products in more than 30 markets across the world. How did she explain her success? 'For every failure,' she said, 'there's an alternative course of action. You just have to find it. When you come to a roadblock, take a detour.'[44]

However many attempts it takes to land, you may have mixed feelings once you have done so. There's the initial thrill of 'Yeah, I've got this', then in the next breath, 'Wow, there's so much to prove now.'

Don't jump up, grab your stuff and jostle your way to be the first off the plane. You still have to collect your baggage and pass through customs before you can explore the destination. Take the time to congratulate yourself on a safe flight, because there is a lot more work to be done now you've hit the ground.

Feet on new ground

Helen Silver AO

Helen Silver has made multiple leaps in a career she describes as 'a serious wander — sideways, upwards, downwards and around'.

She has held senior positions in both the Victorian and Commonwealth public services. As secretary of the Department of Premier and Cabinet in Victoria, she led the Victorian Public Service through significant events; managed the transition of an incoming government and premier; and led negotiations on a range of Commonwealth–state issues.

After 25 years in the public sector, she leapt to the private sector.

'My "leap" from public to private for the first time felt a bit like jumping out of an aeroplane without a parachute. It was completely new ground,' she recalls. 'Someone once used the analogy with me that over time your roots get tight and you need to be re-potted. This particular leap was from pot to paddock!'

There were fundamental differences in the machinery of the business that she knew she needed to manage.

'When I first started in the private sector I didn't understand who I needed to talk to, as unlike the public sector I had no network or close colleagues to seek advice from. I got out the organisation chart and set up meetings with anyone above or below me, and with my peers. I set up meetings with anyone I thought might hit my business or who could benefit from my government experience.

'The fact that I had moved around a lot and had been in senior roles gave me skills that were very relevant in the private sector. Transferable skills like the ability to think laterally and join the dots, get around problems, deal with change, or deal with public exposure, were all useful in the private sector.'

Her advice includes being kind to yourself as you leap. 'Too often you end up blaming yourself when things don't go completely right, rather than focusing on the circumstances and opportunities,' she says. 'Most important is to always keep learning and to understand yourself.'

Manage the destination

When you shift careers, you may assume the role of the adventurous tourist and relish exploring the new world you are in. You may wake up every morning, jump out of bed and think, 'This is awesome!'

Alternatively, either quickly or over time, you may find yourself stuck in a state of culture shock, wondering what on earth you have done. Your expectations of your new role and the reality that unfolds may be completely different. You may feel frustrated and constantly challenged or think, 'I've invested all this time and energy getting here and now I'm not sure this is what I want.'

Whether you are happy playing tourist or are struggling with your new digs, your leap isn't yet complete.

You've landed, but you've only just arrived.

To not find yourself stuck in a permanent transit lounge, there are two key steps to make your leap work: you need to *embed your leap* and then *expand your leap*.

Embed your leap

When you change careers, it can take a while to find your groove. At the start, you'll feel like the new kid on the block. You need to prove to yourself (and perhaps others) that the leap was a good decision. With a new career comes a new language, customs, expectations and challenges. It's natural for this to feel uncomfortable. It's your brain's way of telling you that you are learning something new.

So be kind to yourself and give yourself time to adjust. Explore the new terrain with an open mind, be a bit adventurous and ask lots of questions to get more clarity. In your early days you have the great advantage of being able to ask anything you want, because you're learning.

Also remember to take the time to thank the people who helped you make the leap—your support crew, advisory board and network. It could be a hand-written thank you note or a public acknowledgement through LinkedIn. It's amazing how many people forget this small but important step. If you don't thank people for their efforts, they won't want to help you next time. Remember, you're still in a transition period, so anything can happen and you may need further support.

Whatever career you are now in—whether working for an established organisation or for yourself, in a startup, a not-for-profit or a government agency—there will be expectations about what you do and how you do it. You need to understand what these are quickly, and set about executing on them. It can help to focus on what you want to achieve in the first quarter.

An outstanding book on this subject is *The First 90 Days* by Michael Watkins. While written in an organisational context, it has applicability for lots of different working environments. I have read it multiple times during my career. It sets out the key steps to take to make sure you come through your first 90 days in good shape. 'The actions you take during your first three months in a new job will largely determine whether you succeed or fail,' Watkins explains. 'Transitions are periods of opportunity, a chance to start afresh ... But they are also periods of acute vulnerability, because you lack established working relationships and a detailed understanding of your new role. If you fail to build momentum during your transition, you will face an uphill battle from that point forward.'[45]

Perhaps this sounds harsh, but in my experience of seeing people succeed and fail in new roles I've found it to be true. It is also backed up by various studies that report that 35 to 40 per cent of senior hires fail within their first 18 months.[46] The figures are even higher for lower-level roles. A global talent management survey over three years, involving 5000 hiring managers and 20 000 new employees, found that only 19 per cent of new hires went on to achieve success.[47]

If you take your leap for granted and are not strategic about how you position yourself, build connections or focus your effort, then you'll land face first.

Depending on the career you have moved to, you may or may not have a boss. This can be one of the most critical relationships to nurture. If you get off on the wrong foot, it can be very hard to recover.

Watkins outlines what you need to do to make your relationship with your boss work (though you can apply these tips to your clients too, if you are running a business)[48]:

- Take 100 per cent responsibility for making the relationship work.

- Clarify mutual expectations early and often.

- Negotiate timelines for the work you are doing.
- Aim for early wins in areas important to your boss.
- Seek good feedback from those whose opinions your boss respects.

LAND YOUR LEAP WELL

In your previous career, you were known for something. It's going to take a while to become known in your new career, so consider the following:

1. **Know what success looks like in your new environment.** Set clear goals and know what outcomes need to be achieved, by when and to what standard.

2. **Throw out the old rulebook.** Don't assume that what worked for you in your old career will work in this new environment. Be open to change.

3. **Obsess about presence.** Be present and focused, and look for ways to distinguish yourself from the crowd so you are quickly known for something.

4. **Learn as quickly as you can.** Understand the environment, how it operates, and what may or may not work in this context. Go on a fact-finding mission, seeking out information, insights and contacts.

5. **Build relationships early.** Identify colleagues, stakeholders, clients or suppliers who will be critical in helping you succeed. Get to know their needs and wants, and how what you do can help them. Find the 'makers' — the influencers and connectors — who can best help you navigate the new environment and make progress that matters.

6. **Keep mentally and physical sharp.** Even if you don't feel like you are experiencing culture shock, working in a new environment is mentally and physically draining. Your brain will be in overdrive as it is constantly solving new problems. Find times to rest and recharge.

(continued)

LAND YOUR LEAP WELL (cont'd)

7. **Identify what to scale back to adjust to this new environment.** You may need to establish new routines or create space so you can devote more time to embedding your new role.

8. **Be patient and impatient**. Be patient with yourself as you learn new things; at the same time, be impatient for change and for building success. Don't wait to be told what to do. Figure it out and make it happen.

9. **Reflect constantly.** Move forward and take the time to reflect on progress. Check in with yourself on what is and isn't working. Identify where you may need to shift, adjust or realign your expectations and behaviour.

10. **Reward yourself.** It can be too easy just to move on to the next thing. Take time to celebrate your progress with the people who supported you through the leap.

Expand your leap

You'll know when the leap feels embedded. You'll feel settled, but not too comfortable — just enough to feel like you know your way around the streets. Now is the time to be grateful that you took the risk, invested the effort and made the move to leap. It is such an awesome feeling — well done! This is your Rocky Balboa, Jerry McGuire, Elle in *Legally Blonde* or Peggy Olson in *Mad Men* moment. Celebrate your success and reward yourself for all the effort.

Reflect on the progress you have made and what you have learned along the way. Consider what you might do differently next time, because there will be a next time. When you stay curious and interested with what is happening, you will be able to build on your success.

ASK YOURSELF

- What are my key learnings from this career leap, and what would I do differently next time?

- Am I satisfied with where I am now?

- What else could I do to add value to my work?

- What further learning should I investigate to enhance my career?

- What other relationships could I build to advance my insights and connections?

- Who can I be supporting with their career leap?

- How else could I contribute to those around me?

- What does the next step in my career look like?

Sure, it might feel too soon to be already thinking ahead again, but you always need to be one step ahead in your career!

Remember, things change quickly. Jobs come and go. Throughout my career, the most successful people I have encountered never cruised along, doing the bare minimum. They were always on the lookout for ways to proactively expand the pie.

This shows in research that looks at correlations between proactive personality types and career success. Individuals with a proactive personality tend to look for change in their environment, are not constrained by situational forces, seek out new and different opportunities and show initiative. This study also found that a proactive personality helps people successfully navigate a new career.[49]

Being proactive, showing initiative and taking control of your career are critical to your future success. Remember, only you are in the driver's seat of your career. You are the leader.

Recall the words of Will Durant, an American author, historian and philosopher, channelling Aristotle: 'We are what we repeatedly do. Excellence, then, is not an act, but a habit.'

What if it's not working?

Unlike fairy tales, not all our career stories have a happy ending. There may be times when you have leapt and felt like you've landed on an alien planet. If that's the case, don't make a decision too quickly. Give yourself time to acclimatise. If it seems only to get worse rather than better, dig a little deeper before you hit eject.

ASK YOURSELF

- What isn't working? Is it the role, the people, my boss or other factors?

- Are there aspects of my new career I am enjoying?

- If so, is there a way to tweak what I am doing to do more of that (and less of what I don't like)?

- Is this situation likely to change? To what extent, and can I influence that?

- Is being in this role a potential stepping-stone to something else I'd rather do? If so, is it worth sticking it out for a bit longer?

Remind yourself of why you left your old career in the first place. It's easy to look back on the past fondly and to forget the negatives. There were reasons why you wanted to move on. Are those reasons still valid?

If you discover through those questions that you can influence the outcome and your enjoyment of your new career, then persevere. It will pay off in the end. If, however, you are left with the feeling that you have no control and it won't get any better, then it may be time to make another career leap. Remember, though, flitting from job to job can sometimes damage your reputation, so be sure you stick it out until you know for sure, and always think long term!

Take time to embed

Christine Bartlett

Multiple leaps across her career saw Christine Bartlett move from technical roles to sales to executive leadership. She leapt geographies, industries, business lines and functional areas, and is now operating as a non-executive director sitting on the boards of some of Australia's largest publicly listed companies.

She has found the leaps incredibly energising and discovered the importance of taking time to embed the leap.

'Take time to understand the business, culture and environment you have joined. Don't shoot from the hip,' she counsels. 'I found doing a listening tour very helpful. I then played back to my executive team and the organisation the broad themes that came through. That did a great deal to build trust and credibility.'

She has three main tips for embedding your leap:

1. Understand what skills you have that are transferable. Management/ Leadership skills are transferable. You take your EQ + IQ with you.

2. Make the time to listen and build trust.

3. Don't think you should be expected to have all the answers. The answers will be in the organisation.

CAREER CHECKPOINT

Are you still in mid flight, or have you landed comfortably or with sick bag in hand?

Let's check in to see how you are travelling:

-   Have you completed your pre-flight checklist?

-   Have you boarded the flight ready for launch?

-   Have you sought out an accountability buddy to keep you on track?

If you have landed:

-   Are you putting in effort to embed your leap?

-   Have you checked off the 10 tips to making your leap land well?

-   Are you seeking ways to expand your leap?

-   Have you reflected on learnings from this leap?

10

ADVANCE

WHEN WILL YOU CELEBRATE AND WHAT WILL YOU DO NEXT?

'While living, I want to live well.'
Geronimo

It's standard practice in the United States to award an honorary degree to commencement speakers at colleges and universities. Yet in 2009 Arizona State University decided not to offer the award to then US President Barack Obama. The reason? A spokesperson for the university explained: 'It's normally awarded to someone who has been in their field for some time ... Considering that the president is at the beginning of his presidency, his body of work is just beginning.'[50]

President Obama referenced this incident in his commencement address:

> Now, in all seriousness, I come here not to dispute the suggestion that I haven't yet achieved enough in my life. First of all, Michelle concurs with that assessment. She has a long list of things that I have not yet done waiting for me when I get home.

But more than that, I come to embrace the notion that I haven't done enough in my life; I heartily concur; I come to affirm that one's title, even a title like President of the United States, says very little about how well one's life has been led—that no matter how much you've done, or how successful you've been, there's always more to do, always more to learn, and always more to achieve.[51]

This from someone who has been a lawyer, author, state legislator, US senator and president, yet even he knows there's more he can do!

It's lovely to think that once you've made it to your dream destination you can sit back, sip on a cocktail, bask in the sunshine and finally rest on your laurels.

As I have shown in this book, complacency leads to obsolescence. This applies to products, companies, and even us as humans. So to truly future-proof your career you must always keep your eye out and be ready to advance. Remember, the world—including the world of work—changes rapidly, so you must adapt and constantly forward think and plan.

What's next?

This book is based on the Career Reinvention Cycle. It is a cycle because it never stops. As you come to the end of the last phase, you may find yourself needing to pick up the first phase again.

> The aim of the cycle is not to finish it, but to use it to
> constantly seek ways to improve
> your career and your life.

At some point, you will need to leap to another destination. This shift will occur either because you've decided to embrace change, or because some external force has triggered change.

It can be very easy to ignore the warning signs and to become complacent. Our brain filters out information that doesn't fit with its view of the world, and we tend to seek information that confirms what we believe to be true.

The best way to stay open is to create a practice that helps you to strategically examine how the changing world is going to impact what you do now, and what you could do in the future.

Scan, plan and progress

Most companies undertake an annual strategic planning review during which they look ahead at developments in the external environment and assess how these may impact the organisation's strategy.

One technique used during this review is known as horizontal scanning. This approach focuses on identifying potential threats and opportunities, such as new technologies and disruptive forces in the market. You consider the implications of what's not changing, what is changing and what is constantly changing. You abandon any assumptions about how things should be, and look for 'weak signals' and 'outliers' that may give early warning that the environment is shifting, and that the organisation needs to get ready to respond.

You need to do exactly the same thing with your career. Look for signs by talking to people, reading, digging into ideas you hear about and keeping your finger on the pulse of change.

You also need to set aside dedicated time to review and plan your career, at a minimum every year, although if you are running a business you may need to do it every quarter. This is time to review your progress, reflect on your learnings and identify what's next.

Keeping future focused is about being restless and creatively disruptive, without being agitated and unable to enjoy what you have in front of you.

Enjoy the present and focus on what you have, but always have one foot stepping forward, so you can take control of the future rather than be at its mercy.

Have a life

Planning your future, your career, is not an isolated activity. You need to approach it in the context of your whole life, every aspect of it. As Amy Poehler puts it, 'Your career won't take care of you. It won't call you back or introduce you to its parents. Your career will openly flirt with other people while you are around. It will forget your birthday and wreck your car. Your career will blow you off if you call it too much ...'[52]

Your career matters, and it can become all consuming, yet it is not all of who you are. As one of my clients said to me, 'I want a life that includes a job, not a job that includes a life.'

One of my all-time favourite books is Tal Ben-Shahar's *Happier*. In it he outlines four archetypes of people and how they approach life:

1. The **hedonist** focuses on enjoying the present, ignoring the potential negative consequences of their actions.

2. The **rat racer** is focused so much on potential future gains that they let the present suffer.

3. The **nihilist** enjoys neither the present nor the future.

4. The **happiness** archetype lives secure in the knowledge that the activities they do today will also lead to a fulfilling future.[53]

Adopting the happiness archetype enables you to keep your feet planted in the present, with one eye always looking ahead. You want to celebrate and enjoy the present, while being ready for what comes next.

To do this, it's helpful to take time out to reflect at regular intervals on where things stand in your whole life, including your career. This final activity, exercise 10.1, will help you do that.

Find somewhere peaceful and outside of the office to do this exercise. When you are in a different space your mind shifts and you are able to think differently—both more creatively and more reflectively. Buy a journal for this exercise. It can be incredibly powerful and insightful to look back over the years at how you have responded to these questions and to note what has changed and how you have progressed.

Tip: Don't refer back to your answers from the last review *before* you've completed your current review. If you do, you may unintentionally influence your answers.

After you have reflected on these questions, consider what learnings or changes you want to factor into your new year, your career and your life going forward.

Exercise 10.1: Conduct your career and life stocktake

To check in on your career and life, every year or quarter, answer the following questions.

Career

- What have you achieved this year that you are really proud of?

- What would you do more of or less of next time?

- Do you think your career is on or off track?

- What else do you want to do to progress your career?

- What is changing around you that you need to factor in?

- Is your leadership narrative still current — does it represent who you are and what you stand for?

Connections

- Are you maintaining important connections in your life?

- Are there new connections you'd like to make?

- Are there connections you'd like to strengthen?

- Does your advisory board need tweaking to match where you are right now?

Finances

- Are your financial goals clear?

- Are you on or off track to achieve those goals?

- What additional steps do you need to take to progress?

Learning

- What new skills, knowledge or ideas have you acquired? How are you using them?

(continued)

Exercise 10.1: Conduct your career and life stocktake *(cont'd)*

- What else do you need to know to keep yourself future-proofed?

- In what areas do you need to bolster your expertise?

- What could you learn that is different from your day job?

- What have you learned about yourself recently?

- What have you learned about others recently?

Lifestyle

- Are you spending enough time indulging in pursuits you enjoy?

- What have you done recently that was just for fun?

- What is on your bucket list that you haven't yet ticked off?

Self-care

- Are you getting enough sleep and exercise?

- Are you eating well?

- Are you giving yourself time to recharge?

- Are you using self-care practices (meditation, reflection, a gratitude journal or other activities) that give your mind and body a break?

- Have you recognised and celebrated the breakthroughs and successes you've had?

Service

- How is what you are doing helping others?

- Are you providing support to the community in some way?

- Are you helping people around you, or are you focusing only on your own needs?

Leap into your future

Congratulations! You have completed the Career Reinvention Cycle, during which you have reviewed and reconsidered not just your career but your whole life.

You may have read this book from start to finish or skimmed over some sections. You will have pondered each stage of the cycle and completed some or all of the exercises. Now, for many of you, your career leap is about to start in earnest.

Remember, to really change your career, you must do the work that's needed to make it happen. As you get started, consider the words of the first and three-time recipient of the Pulitzer Prize for Reporting, Herbert Bayard Swope: 'I cannot give you the formula for success, but I can give you the formula for failure—it is: Try to please everybody.'

As you move through the Career Reinvention Cycle there will be people you can please and many you can't. Be true to yourself, while considering others. Be ready to embrace change, and learn through the challenges you encounter. Be bold in the face of adversity and humble when you achieve success.

Liberate your career and, in turn, love your life!

You make it happen
Gorgi Coghlan

How do you transition from being a teacher to working in commercial TV? With a few stepping-stones along the way, that's exactly what Gorgi Coghlan did.

Gorgi's career leaps took her from Year 12 biology teacher, to professional musical theatre, to community television, to TV reporter, to media presenter. She now regularly co-hosts Channel Ten's *The Project*.

'Regret is a far worse emotion to live with than fear,' she says about her willingness to leap. 'You can work through and process fear. You'll always have regret. When you jump, it's certainly scary, but the excitement is in not knowing where you'll land. It's such a cliché, but you really only do get one life. So make the leap and do what you love.'

One of the hardest parts can be trusting yourself and believing in your own talent.

'I had to 100 per cent back myself. I had to process fear and insecurity and tell myself I was worthy, I deserved success, I was going to be okay,' she says.

At one point Gorgi walked away from a lucrative contract as a reporter for a major commercial network because she wasn't happy there—and she didn't have a job to go to. What she did have was a plan, a support network and determination.

'I had a financial plan, a fallback to ease the stress. I was willing to do any work if I had to, but I kept manifesting and believing in what I wanted to achieve. I wrote out my goals, kept a diary and visualised how I wanted my life to be.

'Support from family and friends helped,' she adds. 'One of my biggest drivers was when some people doubted me. This seemed to invigorate me and I used this negative energy to channel my determination. The best thing someone can do is underestimate me!

'I'm so glad I took the leap and risked everything, because otherwise I wouldn't have believed what was possible in my life and my career,' she says. 'What's the worst thing that can happen? You can always start again.'

CAREER CHECKPOINT

Congratulations on navigating your way through the Career Reinvention Cycle! You may be at the 'end', but your work is only just beginning.

In this last stage, you considered these fundamental questions:

- Are you constantly seeking ways to improve your career and your life?

- Have you scheduled and planned your annual or quarterly reflection?

- Are you ready to use the Career Reinvention Cycle again to reinvent and liberate your career, and, in turn, your life?

A MESSAGE FROM MICHELLE

Two of my greatest joys are learning and sharing learning. So writing this book, and being able to share my experiences and the wisdom of others, has been an absolute delight.

If you are committed to liberating your career and really getting fit for the future of work, then it doesn't stop here. The best books (print or digital) are dog-eared, bookmarked and highlighted. They live on as a continuing source of inspiration and reference. My hope is that *Career Leap* is marked up with lots of scribbles and thoughts, collecting much more than dust.

Career leaps don't happen alone. You need a support network to reach your goals. I am always here for that. You can reach me at:

michellegibbings.com

You'll find lots of additional tools, tips and ideas for further advice here too.

And, of course, I'd love to hear how this book has helped you. What worked? What did you find challenging? Where did you leap from and to?

When I'm not writing, I'm speaking, facilitating leadership and team sessions, running training programs and mentoring—all directed towards helping people like you get ready for tomorrow, today.

Let's get liberated together!

Michelle

SOURCES

1 *Harvard Business Review* (2016), 'Globalisation, robots and the future of work: An interview with Jeffrey Joerres, former chairman of Manpower Group', October 2016, pp. 75–9.

2 McKinsey Global Institute (2017), 'A future that works: automation, employment, and productivity', January 2017, pp. 1–148.

3 The McCrindle Blog (2014), 'Job mobility in Australia'.

4 Handy, Charles (2015), 'The Shamrock Organisation', 14 January 2015.

5 Bain & Company (2017), 'The Firm of the Future', April 2017.

6 Muldowney, Susan (2017), 'The rise of the contingent workforce', *Seek Insights and Resources*.

7 Funnell, Antony (2016), 'Is the era of full time work over?', *Future Tense*, ABC Radio National, 7 September 2016.

8 Ismail, Salim, https://www.goodreads.com/author/quotes/8333658. Salim_Ismail.

9 Citrin, James, and Smith, Richard (2003), *The 5 Patterns of Extraordinary Careers*, Three Rivers Press, New York, pp. 30–45.

10 Johnson, Spencer (1998), *Who Moved My Cheese?*, Random House, London, p. 52.

11 Robinson, Ken (2006), 'Do Schools Kill Creativity?', TED Talk.

12 Gilbert, Elizabeth (2015), 'Don't chase your passion and maybe you'll find it', SuperSoul Sessions, 6 November 2015.

13 Baxter, Jennifer (2017), 'The career aspirations of young adolescent boys and girls', Australian Institute of Family Studies.

14 Poehler, Amy (2015), *Yes Please*, Picador, London, p. 219.

15 Burton, L., Westen, D., and Kowalski, R. (2009), *Psychology*, 2nd edn, Wiley, Brisbane, p. 527.

16 Ibarra, Herminia (2015), 'The Authenticity Paradox', *Harvard Business Review*, Jan–Feb 2015, p. 54.

17 Weintraub, Pamela (2010), 'The Dr. Who Drank Infectious Broth, Gave Himself an Ulcer, and Solved a Medical Mystery', *Discover Magazine*, 8 April 2010.

18 McKinsey (2017), 'Where machines could replace humans—and where they can't (yet)'.

19 Davenport, Thomas, and Kirby, Julia (2016), *Only Humans Need Apply: Winners and losers in the age of smart machines*, Harper Business, New York, pp. 19–22.

20 Rao, Anand (2017), 'A strategist's guide to artificial intelligence', *Strategy+Business*, issue 87, 10 May 2017.

21 Futurism (2017), 'Top jobs a decade from now', https://futurism.com/images/will-popular-jobs-future/.

22 Grothaus, Michael (2015), 'The top jobs in 10 years might not be what you think', *Fast Company*.

23 Gray, Alex (2016), 'The ten skills you need to thrive in the fourth industrial revolution', World Economic Forum, 19 January 2016.

24 Schwartz, Barry (2014), 'Is the famous paradox of choice a myth?', *PBS Newshour*, 29 January 2014.

25 de Botton, Alain (2017), https://www.goodreads.com/author/quotes/13199.Alain_de_Botton.

26 Brown, Brené (2013), 'Why your critics aren't the ones who count', 99U Conference, 4 December 2013.

27 Peters, Tom (1999), *The Brand You 50*, Knopf, California.

28 Branson, Richard (2011), *Business Stripped Bare: Adventures of a global entrepreneur*, Penguin, New York, p. 186.

29 Kellogg Insight (2015), 'Fake it until you make it? Not so fast', 3 August 2015.

30 Ibarra, Herminia (2015), 'The Authenticity Paradox', *Harvard Business Review*, Jan–Feb 2015, p. 59.

31 Godin, Seth (2008), *Tribes: We Need You to Lead Us*, Piatkus, London, p. 12.

32 Capps, Rob (2012), 'First impressions: The Science of Meeting People', *Wired*, 20 November 2012.

33 Cuddy, Amy (2016), *Presence: Bringing your boldest self to your biggest challenges*, Orion, London, p. 198.

34 Cuddy, Amy (2016), *Presence*, pp. 224–6.

35 Interview Success Formula (2013), Infographic, https://www.interviewsuccessformula.com/ISF-JobSearchToday972.png.

36 The Undercover Recruiter (2017), 'Why employee referrals are the best source of hire'.

37 Ziglar, Zig, https://www.goodreads.com/quotes/1177933-you-can-have-everything-in-life-you-want-if-you.

38 Garner, Janine (2017), *It's Who You Know: How a network of 12 key people can fast-track your success*, Wiley, Brisbane, p. 140.

39 Sherman, David K., and Cohen, Geoffrey (2006), 'The psychology of self-defense: Self-affirmation theory', *Social Psychology*, vol. 38, p. 184.

40 Sherman and Cohen (2006), 'The psychology of self-defense', pp. 186–7.

41 Sherman, David K. (2013), 'Self-affirmation: Understanding the effects', *Social and Personality Psychology Compass*, Wiley, pp. 834–45.

42 Fox, Jason (2016), *How to Lead a Quest: A handbook for pioneering executives*, Wiley, Brisbane, pp. 72–5.

43 Yaqoob, Tahira (2007), 'Branson takes a leap and flies by the seat of his pants ... but then rips them', *Daily Mail*, 11 October 2007.

44 Biography (2017), 'Mary Kay Ash', https://www.biography.com/people/mary-kay-ash-197044.

45 Watkins, Michael (2003), *The First 90 Days*, Harvard Business School Press, Boston, p. 1.

46 Olson, Matthew S., van Bever, Derek, and Verry, Seth (2008), 'When growth stalls', *Harvard Business Review*, March 2008, p. 10.

47 Contract Recruiter (2017), 'Why 81% of new hires fail, and how to hire for success', Montclair, New Jersey, p. 2.

48 Watkins, Michael (2003), *The First 90 Days*, Harvard Business School Press, Boston, pp. 108–9.

49 Spurk, Daniel, Volmer, Judith, Hagmaier, Tamara, and Kauffeld, Simone, (2017), 'Why are proactive people more successful', University of Technology, Braunschweig University of Erlangen-Nuremberg.

50 Strauss, Valerie (2016), 'In 2009, ASU said President Obama hadn't yet earned an honorary degree. Look who just got one', *Washington Post*, 16 May 2016.

51 'Obama's Commencement Address at Arizona State University', *New York Times*, 13 May 2009.

52 Poehler, Amy (2015), *Yes Please*, Picador, London, pp. 222–5.

53 Ben Shahar, Tal (2207), *Happier: Learn the secrets to daily joy and lasting fulfilment*, McGraw-Hill, New York, pp. 14–16.

INDEX

ability to leap 31–34
accelerate your future career
   133–158
   —launch and landing 135–149
   —what's next? 151–158
acclimatisation 147–149
achieving new career 135–149
activating your future career 85–132
   —entering the market 101–115
   —focus, achieving 117–132
   —identity, new career 87–99
   —influence 101–115
advancing your new career 151–158
Alexander, Marc 124–125
Alice's Adventures in Wonderland 57
ambition 14, 24, 75, 105, 110
anxiety 4, 5, 9, 10, 11, 14, 66, 108
anxious career health zone 10, 11
apathetic career health zone 10, 12
archetypes of people, four 154
architect your future career 37–83
arrogant career health zone 10, 11
AI (artificial intelligence) 46
Ash, Mary Kay 141
ask yourself 24, 64, 66, 94, 123,
   146–147, 148
aspirations 18–19
assessing your current career 1–38

Assisted intelligence 46
athletes 119–120
auditing your personal circumstances
   32–34
   —financial position 33
   —lifestyle expectations 33–34
   —purpose and context 32
   —role requirements 32–33
Augmented intelligence 46
authenticity 93, 104
authenticity paradox 30
automation 6–7, 46–47
Autonomous intelligence 46
autonomy 20, 60, 61

Bartlett, Christine 148–149
Beachley, Layne 65–66
Beckham, Victoria 24
Behavioural Insights team (UK) 113
behaviours 90
   —attractiveness 113
   —changing 113–115
   —ease of contact 113
   —modelling 112
   —sociability 114
   —timeliness 114
Ben-Shahar, Tal 154
Bernieri, Frank 106

Bertrand, John 12–13
Bracks, Steve 74–75
Bradbury, Steven 69
brain 123–124
brand, personal 47, 90
Branson, Richard 90, 135
burnout 5

capabilities 27, 29, 41, 48, 74, 78, 103, 117, 118, 141
career
— current, assessing 1–38
— importance in your life 22, 23, 155
— specifications 60–61
— stocktake 155
— stop signs 4–5
career change elements 43–44
— country 44
— functional role 44
— industry 44
— level 44
— occupation 44
career checkpoints 14, 35, 54, 68, 83, 99, 115, 131–132, 149, 158
career health 7–10
— quiz 8–10
— zones of 8–14
Career Reinvention Cycle 1, 37, 85, 126, 133, 152
celebrating your new career 151–158
choice of progress 57–68
Cialdini, Robert 112, 114
coach, career 109
Coghlan, Gorgi 157–158
comfort levels 40
commentary, internal 24
competencies, future demand for 47–48, 49

competitive advantage 25, 103
confidence 106–107, 128–129
connections see also network; social media
— assessing 155
— building 75
— importance of 22, 23, 67
considering your new career 1–38, 88
constraints 24–25
constructing plans 69–83
courageous actions 25, 29–31
Cuddy, Amy 106–107, 129
culture shock 143
curiosity 18, 51, 107
cynicism 5

decision-making 25, 28, 60
default thinking and behaviour 25, 28
destination 136–137
— desired 50, 51, 58, 60, 61, 63, 69, 72, 73–75, 81, 136, 137, 139
— embedding the leap 143–146
— expanding the leap 143, 146–147
— managing 143–147
— reaching 85–132
development, stages of human 29–30
dialogue, managing your inner 118–121
Do Schools Kill Creativity? 17
down-time, scheduling 124
driver's seat vs autopilot 25
Dweck, Carol 26

effort required for leap 63–66
— market repositioning 65
— networks needed 65

—skill acquisition 65
—stretch, level of 65
—timeframe and 63–66
Emerick, Jim 96
energy, managing your 118, 123–125
Erikson, Erik 29–30
exercises
— 1.1 Career health 8–10
— 2.1 Figure out your why 21
— 2.2 Find your rhythm of life 22–24
— 2.3 Check your mindset 27
— 2.4 Audit your personal circumstances 32–34
— 3.1 How far are you willing to leap? 43–44
— 3.2 Rate your strengths 49
— 3.3 Pinpoint your versatile strengths 50
— 3.4 Hothousing your career leap options 52
— 4.1 Assess your career specifications 61
— 4.2 Assess the level of risk 62–63
— 4.3 Match your timeframe with the effort required 64–65
— 5.1 Plan your learning acquisition program 77
— 5.2 Prepare your master plan 80
— 6.1 Assess your current career identity 92
— 6.2 Write your narrative 97–98
— 9.1 Do your pre-flight inspection 136–137
— 10.1 Conduct your career and life stocktake 155–156
expectations, your own 31–34

expectations of others 14, 16, 25, 29, 30, 119, 120, 143, 144
exploring options 39–55

failure 53, 59, 108, 120, 121, 141, 144, 157
Fallon, Jimmy 102
fear 11, 59, 65–66, 67, 95, 108, 117, 119, 127, 136, 139, 15, 158
feedback 27, 90–92
finance(s)
—assessing 155–156
—financial position 33
—financial security 59–60, 61
—importance of 22, 23
—money in the bank 34–35, 72
First Ninety Days, The 144–145
fitness
—career 7–8
—for the future 1–38
flexibility 17, 20, 24, 31, 33, 47, 49, 60, 61, 71, 72, 74, 78, 79, 129
focus, achieving 117–132
—connections between careers 126
—dialogue, managing inner 118–121
—energy, managing 118, 123–125
—exit, managing 130–131
—negotiating the leap 126–129
—readiness 126–127
—relationships, managing 126, 127–128, 144–145
—resolution to succeed 126, 128–129
—steps to change 125–126
—time, managing your 118, 121–122
—transition 125–126
—tyrannies of progress 118–125

freelancing 47, 53, 103–104
future
— fitness 3–34
— focus 10, 11, 12
— researching 45–47
future, planning for the 151–158
— planning and progression 153
— have a life 153–156
— stocktake exercise 155–156
future-proofing 6–7

Game of Thrones 110–111
gaps to close 76–80
— finances 79, 80
— infrastructure 79, 80
— knowledge 76–79, 80
— legal frameworks 79, 80
— market positioning 80
— network 80
— other activities 80
Garner, Janine 112, 113–114
Godin, Seth 105
gratitude 143, 146

Happier 154
happiness archetype 154
hedonist archetype 154
help
— asking for 13–14, 58, 66, 71,
73, 80, 90, 96, 101, 102, 108,
109, 110, 112, 139, 143, 145
— giving 58, 112, 156
hothousing 51–52
Hutchison, Sandy 139–140

Ibarra, Herminia 30, 96
idea generation 51–52, 58
identity, new career 87–99
— existing 88, 89, 91–92
— feedback 91–92

— market positioning 93
— mis/alignment 91–92
— narrative, writing a new 95–98
— reputation 90–91
— reshaping 98
— shifting 94–95
— understanding your 89, 91–92,
93
— views of others 90–91
influence 101–115; *see also* market,
entering the; network
intelligences 46
intentional thinking 25

Jenkins, Anna 67
Johnson, Spence 6

King, Bronwyn 82–83
knowledge gaps 76–79
knowledge workers 45, 46–47

launching your new career 135–149
— changing your mind 147–148
— destination, managing 143–147
— embedding yourself 143–146,
148–149
— expansion 146–147
— making adjustments 138–139
— managing problems 139–140
— managing relationships 144–145
— pre-flight check 136–138
— settling into new role 140–142
leadership philosophy 96
learning 5, 20, 24, 26, 31, 33–34,
42, 47, 48, 59, 73, 83, 121, 123,
128, 136, 137, 139, 142, 143,
146, 147, 149, 153, 154
— acquisition 76–79
— assessing 156
— importance of 22, 23, 61

liberated career health zone 10, 12, 13–14
lifestyle expectations 22, 23, 33–34
likeability 101–102, 106, 107–108
LinkedIn 103–104, 143
list-making 123

Manners, Anneka 72–73
market, entering the 93, 101–115
 — advisory board 109–112
 — changing behaviour 113–115
 — first impressions 103–104, 106–107
 — help, giving 112
 — likeability 101–102, 106, 107–108
 — networking 102, 103–104
 — online presence 102–104
 — photograph, importance of 104
 — power poses 106–107, 129
 — networking 108–115
 — self-belief 105–106
 — takers, fakers, makers 110–111
Marshall, Barry 39–40
master plan 79–80
Matrix, The 117–118
Matthews, Nigel 30–31
Meet the Parents 16–17
mentors 13–14, 109, 117
mind-mapping 80
mindset(s) 25–31, 126–127
 — default thinking 25
 — growth vs fixed 25, 26–27
 — intentional thinking 25, 28
money, attitude to 22, 23, 33, 34–35, 59–60, 61, 72, 155–156
moonlighting 70–71, 72–73
motivation 89, 122
multi-tasking, fallacy of 124

nanomedicine 47
narrative, writing a new 95–98
Navigator career style 40, 41, 42, 43, 44
negotiation skills 126–129
 — pay 127
 — readiness 126–127
 — relationships, managing 126, 127–128
 — resolution to succeed 126, 128–129
negativity bias 65
network
 — building 80, 108–115
 — ease of association 113–114
 — ease of contact 113
 — scrutinising yourself 109, 112
 — searching for support 109–111
 — shifting your network 109, 113–115
 — takers, fakers, makers 110–111
next move *see* future, planning for the
nihilist archetype 154
nudge unit 112

O'Bama, Barack 151–152
O'Brien, Lisa 78–79
obsolescence 45–47
occupations, disruption by technology 45–47
O'Keefe, Andrew 107–108
options, exploring your 39–55
 — career styles 40–42, 43, 44
 — comfort levels 40
 — filtering 58
 — hothousing 51–52
 — reality check 52–54
 — researching 53
 — shifting 94–95

options, exploring your *(Cont'd)*
—skills vs competencies 47–48, 49
—strengths 48–50
—stretch levels 43–44
—technology, influence of 45–47
over-committing 122, 123

paradox of choice 58
Pareto principle 138–139
passion 17–18
Payne, Carol 21–22
peptic ulcer research 39–40
perfectionism 122, 137
performance 4, 120, 124
personality types 147
Pioneer career style 40, 42, 44
plan, constructing your 69–83, 88
—destination, setting 73–75
—informing your boss 71
—learning and knowledge 76–81
—leaving current job first 72–73
—legal situation 70–71
—master plan 79–80
—mind-mapping 80
—side gig(s) 70–71, 72–73
—timelines 74, 80, 81
—tracking progress 80–83
—transition 70–73
planning ahead 122–123
Poehler, Amy 29
potential, realising your 15–38
—aspirations 18–19
—expectations of others 16–17, 25
—passion 17–18
—purpose 19–22, 32
—rhythm of your life 22–24
—should vs could 16–17
power, sense of, 106–107, 128–129
present, being 121, 145
priorities 59–60, 123, 124, 129

procrastination 58, 72, 79, 119, 122
progress, choosing what to 57–68
purpose 19–22, 32

rat racer archetype 154
readiness to leap 126–127
realising your potential 15–38
regret 157
relationships, managing 126,
    127–128, 144–145
reputation 90–91
—evolved 91
—fictitious 90
—fluid 90–91
—risk of harming 62–63
resigning 130–131
resilience 140
rhythm of your life 22–24
risk 41, 62–63, 75, 83
—financial 62–63
—health/stress 62–63
—relationships 62–63
—reputation 62–63
Roosevelt, Theodore 87

safety net 70
Schwartz, Barry 58
self-affirmation 120–121
self-belief 125, 140, 158
self-care 23, 156
service 23, 146; *see also* help
should vs could 16–167
side gig (s) 70–71, 72–73
Silver, Helen 142
simultaneous careers 72–73
skills 9, 11, 12, 19, 20, 49, 51, 53,
    54, 64, 122, 75, 76, 77, 78, 103,
    104, 105, 107, 108, 122, 126, 141
—transferable 31, 142, 149
—vs competencies 47–48

social media 102–105, 113, 114
— photograph 104
— style and tone 105
social proof 114
specifications, career 60–61
status/power 61
stop signs in career 4–5
stories, career leap 12–13, 13–14,
    21–22, 30–31, 53–54, 65–66, 67,
    72–73, 74–75, 82–83, 94–95,
    107–108, 124–125, 139–140,
    142, 157–158
Stosur, Sam 119–120
strengths
— adaptable 50
— exercises 49, 50
— focus on your 120
— identifying your 48–49
— replaceable 50
— transferable 50
stretch levels 42–44
styles, career 40–42, 43, 44
— Navigator 40, 41, 42, 43, 44
— Pioneer 40, 42, 44
— Surveyor 40, 41, 42, 44
success 133–158
Surveyor career style 40, 41, 42, 44
sweet spot, finding your 58–59

target dates 74
technological change 6–7
thin slicing 106
threats, dealing with 120–121
time, managing your 118,
    121–122
transition to new career 14,
    135–149
tyrannies of progress 118–125

values 5, 19, 21, 22, 29, 30, 88,
    90–91, 120
vulnerability 87, 144

Warren, Robin 39–40
Watkins, Michael 144–145
Watson, Jessica 13–14
what's next? *see* future, planning for
    the
Who Moved My Cheese? 6
why, clarity around *see also* purpose
— starting with 119–22
willingness to leap 31–34
Wilson, Sarah 102–103
work, attitudes to 3–4, 34
Working Girl 105–106
work–life balance 64